Essays on Behavioral Economics

Essays on Behavioral Economics

George Katona

with a contribution
by James N. Morgan

Survey Research Center
Institute for Social Research
The University of Michigan

ISR Code Number 4325

Library of Congress Cataloging in Publication Data:

Katona, George, 1901–
    Essays on behavioral economics.

    Bibliography: p.
    Includes index.
    1. Economics — Psychological aspects — Addresses, essays,
lectures. I. Morgan, James N., joint author. II. Title. III. Title:
Behavioral economics
HB74.P8K29   658.8′342   80-15510
ISBN 0-87944-257-3

Copyright 1980 by The University of Michigan, All Rights Reserved

Published in 1980 by:
The Institute for Social Research,
The University of Michigan, Ann Arbor, Michigan

6   5   4   3   2   1
Manufactured in the United States of America

Jacket Design by Dwayne Overmyer

Contents

2204414

Preface

THIS LITTLE BOOK CONTAINS five essays, four by myself and one by my colleague James N. Morgan, which is reproduced with his permission. Each of my four essays is new, with the exception of a few pages reproduced from a recent publication. The five essays are closely related to each other and are intended as an integrated publication on the essential features of behavioral economics as well as on some major results obtained by this new discipline. Thus, the scope, function, and accomplishments of behavioral economics are presented, as well as its shortcomings, including the problems encountered in 1979. As in my previous books, this one contains theoretical considerations supported by new data.

I wish to acknowledge my great indebtedness to my colleagues at the Survey Research Center of the Institute for Social Research, The University of Michigan, with whom I have continued to collaborate during the last few years when I was officially retired. Thanks are due primarily to James N. Morgan, F. Thomas Juster, Maureen Kallick, and Richard T. Curtin both for ideas that stimulated my thinking and for survey data they collected and placed at my disposal. My former colleague, Burkhard Strumpel, now at the Free University of Berlin, Germany, has influenced my thinking to a large extent, and so has Ernest Zahn of the University of Amsterdam, Holland, especially with respect to Chapter 1 of this book.

As in several previous books, Sylvia M. Kafka has again

used her editorial skills to help me express my ideas. Sincere thanks are also due to Nancy McAllister for her secretarial assistance.

Ann Arbor   George Katona
November 1979

1

The Scope and Function
of Behavioral Economics

During the past three decades numerous empirical studies of economic behavior have been carried out and their theoretical foundation has been clarified. There was a rapid development and articulation of data, theory, and methodology. A new discipline of behavioral economics was emerging.

Behavioral economics has three major features. First, its starting point consists of empirical investigations of the behavior of businessmen and consumers in one country at one time. Generalizations about economic behavior emerge gradually by comparing behavior observed under different circumstances.

Second, behavioral economics focuses on the study of the process of decision making on spending, saving, investing, and the like, rather than on the analysis of such results of behavior as amounts spent, saved, or invested.

Third, the study of the human factor looms large in behavioral economics, which therefore has also been called psychological economics. Behavioral economics measures and analyzes such psychological antecedents of economic activities as the motives, attitudes, and expectations that influence decisions in economic matters.

In all these respects, behavioral economics differs greatly from the procedures of classical economics, which deduces principles of economic behavior from features of human nature assumed to be valid at all times and in all cultures. Behavioral economics also differs from econometric studies, which are commonly begun by setting up general models and then testing derivations from the models by confronting them with statistical data. The results obtained in behavioral studies have sometimes differed greatly from traditional economic insights, as will be shown later, and have contributed to the understanding and the prediction of economic developments.

At present, when a fairly large body of findings and generalizations from studies of economic behavior is available, there is a need to outline the scope and function of the new discipline. The question as to the kind of studies or subdisciplines belonging to behavioral economics may be answered in two ways, either in an expansive manner by defining behavioral economics as the study of all forms of behavior that relate to the economy, or by restricting behavioral economics to the forms of economic behavior that are traditionally major subjects of economic investigation. We begin by enumerating first those studies of behavior that undoubtedly fall in the province of behavioral economics and then expand the list to neighboring fields.

Subdisciplines of Behavioral Economics

Studies of Consumer Behavior. Included in these studies are analyses of the process of spending for necessities, services, and durable goods (homes for owner occupancy, automobiles, appliances) that reflect orientation toward the future. Various aspects of market research, such as an analysis of brand loyalty or the impact of advertising, also belong in this subdiscipline.

Studies of Saving Behavior. Analyses of planned as well as contractual and residual saving, of the choice between spending and saving, and of the choice among various saving media (banks, securities, etc.) are included here, as are studies of plans to retire and of decisions to retire early or late.

Studies of Business Behavior (entrepreneurial behavior). Analysis of decision making by business firms is undertaken within this subdiscipline, with special reference to motives and goals, short-term as well as long-term, and to participation in decision making. Studies of risk taking and the influ-

4

ence of uncertainty on behavior are of particular interest. Herbert A. Simon's extensive studies of the process of decision making by business firms, closely linked with the psychology of problem solving, are outstanding examples of research on how business firms arrive at decisions.

Studies of Earning Income. The field includes not only the study of what uses are made of income (and other available resources), but also the process of striving for income through occupational choice, decisions about career, greater or lesser effort, longer or shorter working hours, additional training, and so forth. More attention must be paid to decisions about second jobs and about women entering the labor force.

Studies of Economic Behavior in Different Market Systems. Capitalist or free market economies differ greatly with respect to the extent of government control and its acceptance by the people. Studies of similarities and differences in economic behavior in, say, Western Europe and the United States contribute to the process of arriving at generalizations on principles of economic behavior. Little has been done as yet to expand these studies to a comparative analysis of economic behavior in communist countries or in developing countries.

Studies of Politico-Economic Behavior. Comparative studies of economic behavior reflect the relationship between politics and economics. In addition, many studies investigate attitudes toward taxation and various government programs and their impact on behavior.

If behavioral economics were to be defined as encompassing studies of all forms of behavior that influence the economy, further research areas would belong in that discipline. Such a broad classification is inadvisable because it would result in the inclusion of scholars who do not see themselves as behavioral economists. Nevertheless, we shall mention two important related areas of inquiry:

Studies of the Process of Working. Included here are studies of motives to work and such often conflicting goals as

5

striving for higher income, fringe benefits, proper working environment, participation in management, and self-fulfillment.

Studies of Organizational Behavior (often called organizational psychology, or research in human relations in institutions). These very extensive studies analyze primarily the relation between organizational structure and human performance, organizational change and the impact of leadership.

On Findings of Behavioral Economics

Studies of behavioral economics were first undertaken as a consequence of two new developments that provided a need for such studies, as well as the possibility to carry them out. During and shortly after World War II the proportion of "affluent" consumers who acquired discretion in spending and saving increased greatly in the United States. Many more families than at earlier times had some discretionary income available after completing their expenditures for necessities. Thus, consumers were in a position to undertake discretionary expenditures, especially for durable goods, and were confronted with a much wider choice among expenditures than ever before. Discretionary expenditures can be postponed or can be undertaken before the goods and services purchased are urgently needed. Being attracted by a good or service plays a great role in decisions to make these expenditures. Therefore, in an affluent society characterized by "more for many" rather than "much for a few" (see Katona, 1964), motives, attitudes, and expectations play a much greater role than in a poor society in which consumer expenditures are a function of income. The latter traditional principle of economic theory had made it possible to effectively exclude consumers from economic analysis because change in personal income, the assumed sole determinant of consumer expenditures, was frequently thought to depend on decisions by the business sector rather than the consumer sector.[1] When,

however, what may be justifiably called consumer investment expenditures[2] became the most significant factor influ-
encing business trends, it was necessary to undertake studies
of antecedents of consumer behavior other than income or
ability to buy.

At about the same time a new method became available to
carry out quantitative studies of the results of consumer
behavior as well as to measure consumers' motives, attitudes,
and expectations. The sample interview survey made it possible to collect economic-financial data, demographic data, and
psychological data from the same individuals who fell in the
sample and to relate the different kinds of data to one
another. Thus, to give just one example, expenditures on
automobiles were related not only to the income but also to
the age and the expectations of the purchasers. In addition,
provided the sample was representative of all consumers, the
survey method yielded aggregate data both on economic
activities — for instance, the number of cars bought in a given
period — and on consumer attitudes — for instance, on the
proportion of optimists or pessimists during that period (and
especially on the changes in car purchases and in optimism or
pessimism). In contrast, traditional economic analysis, not
making use of survey data, had at its disposal only aggregate
data on consumer expenditures, which were available from a
variety of records, and no quantitative data at all on economic motives or expectations.[3]

The purpose of empirical studies on the relation of consumer expenditures and savings to attitudes and expectations
far exceeded the collection of descriptive data on the economy. These studies opened the way to answer the question of
"why" — why people increased the amounts they spent on durable goods as well as why they voted as they did, for
instance. From the outset, the researchers intended to test
basic principles of economic theory by applying psychological hypotheses in addition to economic hypotheses to economic behavior. Some of the implications of behavioral

7

studies based on surveys will be recounted here by enumerating a variety of problems studies by the author over the past 30 years.

1. Understanding Economic Trends. We shall refer here to just two important examples. Following a sharp increase in the purchase of cars and other durables after the end of World War II, the great majority of American families experienced 25 years in which the quantity of the goods they owned increased and their standard of living improved. Why was there, following widespread large purchases, no saturation with goods and services at an earlier date, say in the mid-1950s or early 1960s? Very briefly, because optimistic and confident people steadily expanded their wants and raised their levels of aspiration after they had accomplished the goals set earlier (Katona, 1964 and 1971).[4] Periods of rising demand were interrupted only by occasional short recessions between 1945 and 1970.

In the spring of 1973 substantial increases in food prices shocked the American people, and the government's attempts to fight inflation by raising interest rates reinforced the widely felt malaise. The phenomenon of the generalization of affect — both good and bad feelings tend to spread from one area to other areas (see Katona, 1964, p. 160 ff.) — manifested itself. Expectations of bad times and of a recession became widespread without modifying inflationary expectations even before the sudden news of the oil embargo surprised the American people late in 1973.

Behavioral economics collects data that explain the trends predicted by the measurement of attitudes and expectations. To say that at a given time expectations point toward an upswing (or downswing) is not enough. The reasons for the changes in expectations need to be known. Such information is regularly supplied by the survey data collected.

2. Predicting Economic Trends. While the most common forecasting methods extrapolate past trends, the measurement of changes in people's expectations provides a method of forecasting that is particularly suitable to discerning in advance probable cyclical turning points. Feeling better or worse off, expecting to be better or worse off, and notions and expectations of an improvement or deterioration in economic trends, as well as favorable or unfavorable evaluations of market conditions, were chosen as an interrelated set of attitudinal factors which served as advance indicators of prospective changes in consumers' discretionary expenditures.

The Index of Consumer Sentiment was constructed from such data and since 1955 has been regularly published by the Survey Research Center several times a year (see Katona, 1975, Chapters 5 and 6). As shown in Chart 1, the Index turned down long before the onset of each of the postwar recessions. For example, the deepest postwar recession of 1974–75 was indicated by increased pessimism and reduced confidence early in 1973 at a time of high and rising demand and was confidently predicted long before the recession set in (and before OPEC initiated the oil embargo).

Prior to the onset of economic upturns, the performance of the Index was satisfactory, but the time lag between the change in the attitudinal indicators and in spending or saving was shorter than it was before downturns. In periods of little economic change, attitudes fluctuated little and the Index did not perform better than extrapolative forecasts. The importance of attitude measures at these times consisted of the reassurance they provided that major changes were *not* imminent.

These studies indicate that (a) changes in consumer attitudes and expectations are measurable, (b) attitudes and expectations represent intervening variables modifying overt behavior, (c) changes in optimism and pessimism and therefore in willingness to buy have a great impact on discretionary expenditures, and (d) changes in consumer expenditures on durable goods have a substantial influence on general economic trends.

3. Analysis of the Consumer's Role. Traditionally, busi-

9

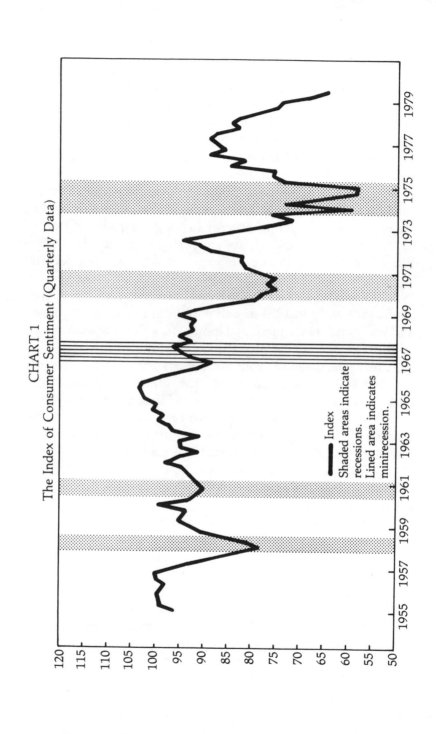

CHART 1
The Index of Consumer Sentiment (Quarterly Data)

Index
Shaded areas indicate recessions.
Lined area indicates minirecession.

ness investment in plants and machinery has been considered the major factor in economic progress as well as the most volatile economic process, initiating upswings and downswings in the economy. After the end of World War II a consumer economy developed in which consumer investment expenditures assumed the leading role in economic growth and in bringing about cyclical change. Consumer attitudes thus provided advance indications of what would happen in the entire economy, even though they were clearly related to just one, relatively small part of GNP. It has been demonstrated and is widely accepted by students of the business cycle that it was the consumer who plunged the American economy into a recession in 1958, 1970, and 1974. Similarly, the consumer was called the hero in 1959, 1971, and 1975.[5] Thus it was justified at an early date to speak of the "powerful consumer."[6] The large fluctuations in consumers' investment expenditures originated in their attitudes and expectations rather than in income changes or marketing and advertising efforts by business firms.

4. *Attitudes toward and Behavior during Inflation*. Descriptions of periods of inflation that have occurred over many centuries in many countries and theories of inflation emphasize that excessive demand represents the major feature of inflation. The old adage about "more money chasing fewer goods" may serve to illustrate the core of diverse theories of inflation and also the widely used substitution of the behavior of money for the behavior of consumers and businessmen. This is true irrespective of whether inflation is attributed to "demand-pull" due to government deficits, credit expansion, or growth of money supply, or to "cost-push" due to rapid wage increases.

Observations of the American people's attitudes and behavior between the end of World War II and the 1970s revealed, however, that under the impact of general price increases, two phenomena were clearly present:

a) Most people felt worse off and tended to spend less than

11

at times of little inflation. Even people whose income rose more than prices complained about being deprived of enjoying what they considered the well-deserved fruits of their labor.

b) Widespread uncertainty arose so that people in general felt the need to save more than before in order to be able to pay for necessities in the future when they would cost more.

The result of accelerated price increases, therefore, was the spread of pessimism, of reduced expenditures for durables and other postponable goods and services, of economizing and saving more (see Katona, 1960, 1964; and Juster and Wachtel, 1972).

On certain occasions, however — in 1950 under the impact of military defeats in Korea, in 1973 when food prices sky-rocketed (see point 1 above), and in 1977–79 for one-family houses and automobiles because of inflationary expectations (see point 5 below) — a different form of behavior emerged. Instead of circumspect buying and shopping around, some consumers and businessmen turned to buying in advance of their needs, stocking up, and even hoarding in order to beat inflation. Analysis of the antecedents of such behavior — changes in motives, attitudes, and expectations — made it possible to shed light on the circumstances under which the one form of behavior (saving more) or the other form of behavior (spending more) was predominant (see Katona, 1978).

5. *The Law of Demand.* This basic principle of economic theory says that the higher the price, the smaller the demand, and vice versa. Among the many instances in which the law was confirmed, just one recent experience will be mentioned. Following a reduction in 1978 in the price of airplane tickets, both for domestic and international travel, there was a substantial increase in air travel. But in other instances the law has been contradicted. In 1977–79 consumers responded to large increases in the prices of one-family houses and auto-

12

mobiles by stepping up the rate of their purchases because they expected further substantial price increases in the future. Attitudes and expectations functioned as variables intervening between stimulus (change in prices) and response (the extent of demand). As will be shown in Chapter 5 (see Chart 5), behavioral research has provided quantitative indications of underlying motivational factors. Expectations were at that time the major factor shaping the demand for the two largest purchases a family ever makes — a house for their own occupancy and a car.

6. *Saving.* Beyond the fairly common occurrence of contractual and residual saving that do not result from strong motives to save, large additions to savings and reserve funds have been found to be common only among middle-aged families with substantial income and large assets. Although the desire to accumulate financial reserves arises early, most younger and lower income families "save" by buying a house for their own occupancy and buying durable goods, contributing to social security and private pensions, and not by putting money in banks or securities. Wealth, rather than reducing the propensity to save, tends to raise the amounts saved because of rising levels of aspiration and because established habits of saving tend to continue.

7. *Rational Behavior.* In contrast to the emphasis of economic theory on rationality, defined as weighing available alternatives and choosing the alternative that maximizes utilities or profits, behavioral economists found a common occurrence of habitual behavior — doing what has been done in the past, following established routines and following leaders — occasionally interrupted by genuine decision making. Only in those relatively few instances when the decision really matters do strong motivational forces arise that lead businessmen and consumers to proceed in a circumspect manner. Even then the alternatives considered are usually restricted according to their attitudes and expectations, and a satisfying course of action is chosen rather than one that will optimize

the outcome (see Simon, 1957 and 1978; and also Katona, 1953 and 1975, pp. 297 ff.). Simon's theory of bounded rationality takes into account people's limited ability to make comparisons and to see into the future; it therefore differs greatly from traditional theory and also from more recent attempts to formulate a theory of probabilistic choice.

Recent writings on "rational expectations" indicate how some theorists make observation and measurement of expectations unnecessary by assuming that expectations are formed rationally. It is assumed that what the prevailing expectations are can be deduced from such factors as past trends, the consideration of past forecasting errors, and all information available about future events at a given time. This extreme example of how belief in rationality serves to deny the need for empirical research is contradicted by findings that businesses and consumers often base their expectations on a complex set of information as they perceive and reorganize it, rather than on an extrapolation of past events or a "rational" consideration of news.[7]

These references to results of behavioral studies that provided new insights into economic processes could be expanded, even with respect to the analysis of consumer behavior. No mention has been made, for instance, about progress in understanding the buying process or decision making within the family. More generally, business behavior has not been discussed even though the psychological analysis of economic behavior began with studies of business (see Katona, 1951), and they play a large role among the current endeavors of the Survey Research Center. Finally, it should be recalled that the author's studies of economic behavior during the prosperous 25 years following World War II were summarized by an attempt to compare economic processes in the United States with those in Western Europe, and to derive some generalizations by an analysis of similarities and differences in different countries, including studies of the acquisition of income and of motives to work (Katona, Strumpel, and Zahn, 1971). Rather than continuing with such references,[8] we turn to the more general need for expanding the scope of behavioral economics.

Behavioral Economics in Changing Times

An urgent need to expand the scope of behavioral economics arose in the 1970s. Since the possibilities of conducting experiments in the economic area are limited, the availability of controlled observations of behavior under changed circumstances greatly enlarges the possibility of arriving at generalizations. The following discussion should serve to illustrate that the measurement of attitudes and expectations may yield consequences relevant for an assessment of the economic outlook over several years, beyond predictions of short-term prospects.

The author has characterized the new trends that began to develop toward the end of the 1960s as a new economic era (Katona and Strumpel, 1978). In the quarter century from 1945 to 1970 there was rapid growth and an unprecedented, strong improvement in the standard of living of masses of people. In that era people's expectations, aspirations, and desires for more consumer goods, better jobs, and greater income security were largely fulfilled. As reported before, optimistic and confident Americans responded to a fulfillment of their wishes by raising their levels of aspiration. In contrast, growth was slow in the era that started in the 1970s, inflation was rapid, and unemployment was high. The new era developed and sustained itself because people's beliefs had changed substantially. In listing some major features of the underlying attitudes in the 1970s, we refrain here from documenting them since this has been done elsewhere (Katona and Strumpel, 1978).

Crisis of Confidence. Mistrust of government and especially of its ability to alleviate economic evils, as well as of big business and experts in general has become especially pro-

15

nounced. The deterioration of confidence in the government was shown to have begun at the time of the war in Vietnam, was strengthened during the Watergate crisis, and intensified again because of rapid inflation during the Carter presidency in 1978–79 (see Chart 4 in Chapter 5).

Disorientation and Confusion. Notions became widespread that "nobody" knew why rapid inflation, substantial unemployment, and frequent economic fluctuations had come about and how they could be remedied.

Scaling Down Aspirations. The belief became commonly shared that the best that could be hoped for was slowing down price increases, slightly reducing unemployment, and achieving small increases in real income. People began to doubt the possibility of enduring growth of the economy and a steady improvement in their situation.

Uncertainty and Volatility. These factors became major characteristics of both economic behavior and economic attitudes.

In all these respects, quantitative data indicate great differences between the 1970s and the two preceding decades. In the 1950s and the early 1960s the great majority of people trusted the government — for instance, they believed that "what goes up will come down" because the government would act to arrest inflation — thought they understood what was happening in the economy and had high aspirations. Measures of the limited uncertainty in the earlier era and heightened uncertainty in the new era will be presented in Chapter 4.

Behavioral economics, developed in an era of spreading affluence and optimism, is confronted with new tasks in an era of limited growth and uncertainty. Studies of economic behavior in the new era had to be broadened to encompass aspects of political behavior since political considerations contributed greatly to the absence of confidence in government.[9] Studies of attitudes toward the degree to which government should intervene in economic affairs had to be

16

undertaken jointly with those of the increased value attributed to the environment — concern with pollution, misgivings about nuclear waste, and the like. The consideration of changes in the work ethic stemming from the greater value placed on conditions of work and self-fulfillment through one's job likewise became an integral part of the analysis of economic behavior.

International and intercultural comparisons of economic behavior are of great significance in the new economic era. Similarities in trends between the United States and Western Europe prevail with respect to the experience of slow growth and sizable unemployment as well as to the development of less optimistic expectations. But there have also been great differences in developments. For instance, in Germany inflation was rather slow, the currency strong, workers' participation in management widespread, and a variety of economic functions of the government were generally accepted.

The role of business investment in particular has been different in Germany and in the United States during the last 30 years. The proportion of GNP devoted to investment in plants and machinery as well as the proportion of personal income saved were much larger in Germany than in the U.S. In contrast, in the U.S. a consumer economy developed in which purchases of durables, rather than changes in business investment, triggered upswings as well as downswings in the economy. The differences in the rate of saving in the two countries have been shown to have resulted primarily from the continuous increase in installment debt in the U.S. and the reluctance to resort to installment buying in Germany (see Katona, Strumpel, and Zahn, 1971, and Strumpel, 1975). Over the last few years, however, an American-type consumer economy has begun to make inroads in Germany, while in America there is some question about the continuation of the major role of consumer durable goods expenditures.

By the late 1970s, the proportion of American families

17

owning a car reached 85 percent, 40 percent of families owned two or more cars, and 70 percent lived in their own one-family houses. The question arises whether the rapid growth in home and car ownership can continue at a time when growth in population and in real incomes has slowed down.

Up to now there have been no signs of a reduced attraction of home ownership or car ownership. But consumers are increasingly aware of their high costs. The sharply rising prices of houses and cars and the high interest rates cause hardship and complaints, and dissatisfaction with high real estate taxes and with high gasoline prices is common.

In view of the energy crisis, less consumption of goods that require the use of great amounts of energy and other natural resources would be very welcome. Some change in subjective priorities has already taken place. Improvement in well-being tends to be centered today to a lesser extent than in the past on the ownership of a larger number of goods and more on the quality of the goods — including their durability and lower maintenance costs — and on the quality of life in general. New measures of social indicators show that satisfaction with various domains of life — family and health as well as economic well-being — and that happiness in general have not increased in the past decade when, on the whole, real incomes have advanced. Although the well-to-do are more satisfied than the poor, the general level of satisfaction is not any higher in rich than in poor countries. Economic satisfaction is increasingly a function, not of the number of goods owned, but of the environment. There has been growing concern with matters that do not depend solely on the amount of money a family has — health, schools, safety, pollution, conditions of work. Security, a greatly-desired goal, has acquired a broader meaning beyond job security and the size of available savings. Security is felt to be threatened by a variety of developments which many consumers feel helpless to change, such as inflation, absence of safety, inadequate health care, lack of proper environmental standards. At the same time when more and more people feel entitled to receive an adequate income, their subjective control over their own economic fate has diminished.

A crucial factor responsible for the improvement in well-being during the first two decades following World War II was the widespread striving for betterment, improvement, and progress. Apparently, striving for progress is a prerequisite for favorable economic trends. But it is not necessary that people strive for the same goals in the future as they did in the past. A redefinition of what is meant by progress has already begun. The process of broadening the concerns and goals from material goods possessed by the family to the environment and the quality of life that affect one's group, community, or the entire economy represents a psychological shift that is and will be of great importance in the future.

The need for psychological studies of economic behavior has grown in the last few years when uncertainty, volatility, and turbulence have characterized the economy. It may suffice to point to the unusually frequent and substantial fluctuations of the foreign exchange markets to indicate that need for a better understanding of the motives and expectations of the managers of large financial assets as well as of business managers in general. Studies designed to arrive at such an understanding would doubtless be difficult to conduct, but the time has come to undertake them and thus to broaden the scope of behavioral economics.

The Functions of Behavioral Economics

What are the functions of behavioral economics? The following enumeration of its major functions appears to be valid irrespective of whether behavioral economics is viewed in a rather restricted or a very extended manner.

1. Understanding Economic Trends in One Place at One Time. Statistical data compiled from records (e.g., on changes in GNP, in retail sales, or in corporate profits) serve the purpose of helping us understand what has happened in the economy. But subjective data, for instance, on changes in felt well-being and in expectations, supplement the data derived from records in a crucial manner. People's perceptions about whether their own or their country's economic situation has improved or deteriorated contributes to an assessment of data taken from records. Consumers' and business managers' opinions about why certain things have happened shed light on the decision-making process regarding increasing or decreasing investment expenditures.

2. *Predicting Economic Trends.* Data on changes in economic attitudes and expectations as well as in aspirations and values of consumers and businessmen serve as an important predictive instrument, especially at times of impending reversals of economic trends.

3. *Assisting Economic Policy.* Whether or not an economic policy measure, either planned or initiated, is accepted or rejected by those whose actions may influence its success or failure is of great importance. Behavioral economics must contribute to "conditional forecasts" by analyzing the probable behavioral response to different policies and developments (e.g., to higher interest rates). In addition, studies of the reasons for the acceptance or rejection of a new policy may supply information that can serve the purposes of changing the measure as well as of explaining it to the public. This is true of government policy regarding inflation, taxes, and new or changed economic programs, as well as of new policies instituted by business firms.

4. *Improving Economic Theory.* Studies of the circumstances under which generalizations about economic processes are or are not valid serve not only the function of making economics more realistic, but also the function of improving economic theory. Information derived through the measurement of expectations and the determination of their origins belongs in the mainstream of economics. The new approach

supplements the traditional approach to economic theory. This is true with respect to basic issues relating to rationality or the law of demand as well as to such specific problems that have surfaced during the last few years as the relation of unemployment to inflation and the impact of restricted prospects for growth. The ultimate goal of the full integration of traditional economic theory with generalizations established by behavioral economics has yet to be achieved.

Notes

1. During the last 10 years or so family incomes also increased because many more women than before decided to enter the labor market. The substantial increase in available jobs resulted, of course, primarily from decisions by the business sector.

2. This expression is useful because it points to the similarities between business investment and consumer investment: both require the consideration of future trends, both are usually undertaken by incurring debt, and both are commonly discretionary and depend to a large extent on desires and wishes rather than urgent needs (see Morgan, 1958).

3. Survey data provide a variety of measures of results of behavior for which data from records are not available. This is true, for example, of the proportion of families owning two or more cars and of those buying used cars, not to mention such well-known items as price indices and unemployment data for which government surveys provide continuous information. In the many instances in which data on consumer expenditures or savings are available from records as well as from surveys, the former are, of course, superior because survey data are subject to sampling and reporting errors. But the former cannot be easily related to demographic and attitudinal data. The same is true of information about voting behavior. Election results are compiled from records, but surveys alone provide information on how different demographic groups vote as well as how people with different attitudes vote.

4. Thus, a psychological theorem developed by Kurt Lewin (1944) on the basis of small-scale experiments on the dynamics of aspirations was applied to economic behavior.

5. A few data may be reproduced here, as compiled by the Federal Reserve Bank of St. Louis *Review,* June 1976. From the previous peak to the recession trough, in 1958, the real GNP fell by 3.2 percent and the number of cars sold in the U.S. fell by 31.7 percent in 1958; in 1974 these figures were 6.6 percent and 42.6 percent, respectively. The increases from the trough through the fourth subsequent quarter were 7.1 percent in real GNP and 39.6 percent in auto sales after 1958, and 7.1 percent and 31.1 percent, respectively, after 1974.

6. This was the title of a book published by the author in 1960, even though at that time there was no consumerism movement and individual consumers were, and still are, rather powerless at the market place.

7. How rational expectations may differ from actual expectations as determined by empirical studies may be illustrated by referring to Milton Friedman, who in his Nobel lecture implied his acceptance of the concept of rational expectations and stated a priori what the expectations were at certain times. He said, for instance, that "in the immediate post-World War II period, prior experience was widely expected to recur... The expectation in both countries [U.S. and U.K.] was deflation" (1977, p. 465). But we know from extensive surveys conducted under the direction of the author, the results of which were published in the 1946 and 1947 volumes of the *Federal Reserve Bulletin* (under the titles "National Survey of Liquid Assets" and "Survey of Consumer Finances"), that after World War II ended the American people were elated and optimistic, expected good times to come, and planned to buy many things. In contrast to some experts, they did not expect the resumption of the deflation of the 1930s. Consumers and businessmen behaved in line with their opinions and expectations, and there was no postwar recession.

Nevertheless, in the absence of any empirical studies of the futures markets, the possibility cannot be denied that the theory of rational expectations may apply to those markets in which the participants search extensively for information.

8. There have recently been some attempts to link economics and psychology, which are not discussed in this paper. Scitovsky, in his work on the psychology and economics of motivation (1976), and Solomon and Corbit in their report (1978) on the "opponent-

process theory of motivation," have relied primarily on conditioned reflex and drive psychology. In contrast, the starting point of this author (Gestalt psychology and cognitive psychology) reflects the belief that higher mental processes are involved in economic behavior (see Katona, 1951).

9. Over the last two decades, political scientists at the Institute for Social Research have developed an Index of Trust in Government, constructed from survey questions not related to the economy. This Index traces the decline of confidence in the presidency (see Miller, 1974). Miller has also shown that distrust of the President is related to, but not identical with, unpopularity of the incumbent or distrust of authority. People's evaluations of the institution of the presidency have suffered because they disapproved of the manner in which presidents dealt with such great problems as Vietnam, racial issues, student unrest, or misuse of power.

2

A Realistic Economics
of the Consumer
Requires Some Psychology

James N. Morgan

How can we have more realistic theory and research about economic behavior without an explosion of variables or a retreat into crass empiricism?[1] One method is to start with the main and most obvious ways in which a simple one-dimensional utility-maximization theory fails to reflect reality. I shall discuss five that I think are most crucial:

1. *Multiple Motives.* A person with a set of needs or desires faces a variety of products or services, each with multiple attributes. The utility of any one product or service is actually a complex function of its attributes.

2. *Group Decisions.* In the family and probably even in the firm, there are several individuals with differing patterns of needs, trying to achieve some consensus about what to do. Elements of a power struggle mix with altruism. Communication may fail.

3. *Uncertainty.* Most decisions involve commitments about an uncertain future. The length and size of such commitments can be expected to vary with the degree of uncertainty about the future.

4. *Ignorance of Facts.* Knowledge about the range of alternatives and their actual prices and qualities is not readily available to most of us without work and expense. Decisions must be made about investment in information, and there are problems of decision making when the facts are *not* all known.

5. *Confusion.* Economic decisions require an understanding of economic principles to know which facts are needed, and what to do with them. The great policy issue of whether consumers need more facts or more protection hinges on whether they would know what to do with the facts if they

27

had them; whether consumers are not just informable, but educable!

Multiple Motives

Theoretical writings by Kelvin Lancaster (1968, 1971) have discussed the implications of the fact that any commodity has a number of characteristics which must be merged with a number of needs of the individual to produce a desirability (utility?) indicator. There have been some statistical attempts to tease out shadow prices of attributes of cars or houses or jobs from the market prices of those with varying combinations of attributes. This puts a heavy burden on the data in view of various supply conditions and the need for assuming all or large blocks of consumers have the same tastes.

What seems to be missing in all this is sufficient attention to the differing motives or needs of the consumers. Tibor Scitovsky's book, *The Joyless Economy*, focuses on the need for novelty and stimulation as well as comfort and satiety, but surely we would want to add desire for power over others, affiliation with others, and achievement against obstacles as also motivating much of our behavior.

Perhaps the most useful paradigm for making use of motives is that of John Atkinson, who argues that there is an incentive level of each need, depending on how much it has already been satisfied (declining marginal utility), a basic level of importance of that motive, and a subjective probability that some course of action (acquiring a product?) will indeed produce some of that sort of satisfaction.[2]

If we are primarily interested in *change* in behavior, then we may want to focus on two things: the way experience changes people's notions about the probability that some particular product, activity, or choice will produce satisfaction; and the extent to which aspiration levels tend to be satiated on the one hand, or to rise with each achievement on the other.

28

For example, the life insurance provisions of the Social Security System did not eliminate private life insurance, and some argue that it made adequate provision possible and actually stimulated additional private insurance to make the coverage really sufficient. A study of the impact of private pensions when they were initiated, largely involuntarily, indicated that if anything they raised aspirations for a truly adequate retirement income and increased private saving. (See Katona, 1965.)

Focusing on personal motives and perceived paths for satisfying them may well be a more fruitful approach to consumer behavior than focusing on attributes of products. People's perceptions and subjective probabilities surely change more rapidly than product characteristics, and people's aspiration levels may also change under the impact of experience, success, failure, or even persuasion.

Group Decision Making

If we have done little on how multiple motives combine with multiple product attributes and with some probabilities to generate expected utilities, our ability to deal with group (family) decision making is even more deficient. Kenneth Arrow proved some time ago the impossibility of any simple social welfare function, and the same problems arise with a family attempting to develop a family set of preference orderings.

Since families do make decisions, a majority of them sufficiently satisfactory so that the family stays together, we might ask whether we can develop some notions about their methods. There are possible contributions from psychology on power, conformity and altruism, from sociologists on roles and role expectations, and from economists on multilateral trade and bargaining. Market researchers have asked directly who made the decision and have found the usual ego bias in the answers, plus a tendency to conform to social roles

29

as to who is expert in what — women on style, color, and the household, men on mechanics and the car. A study by Elizabeth Wolgast that looked at who could predict what the family would do found the women predicted better, even in the male areas.

We could surely use more studies of communication and consensus in the family — who knows that others want, does actual agreement go along with perceived agreement? And where there are differences, or disagreements, we could perhaps be studying the relative role of power and affiliation in reaching acceptable compromises. We do not, of course, have a good theory to handle decision making when affiliation motives dominate. Indeed, one of C.S. Lewis' funniest episodes in the *Screwtape Letters* is one where everyone tries to do what the others want, and they all end up angry. Since the family is the main source of support for otherwise dependent members of society, overwhelmingly more important than social security and welfare, its stability is an important public policy issue.[3]

Uncertainty

For more than a quarter of a century now, the main work on the actual effects of uncertainty on the consumer has been that of Katona. Coming to this problem with a background in psychology *and* economics, Katona decided that since the crucial economic behavior for economists was spending and committing funds, and since the major dynamic explanatory variable was probably uncertainty about one's personal financial future and about the country's economy, one should start investigating the link between events, mass attitudes, and mass consumption expenditures.

It was clear years ago that changes in consumer investment expenditures were large, dramatic, and more difficult to predict than changes in business investment expenditures. It tells us something of the difficulties of using psychology in economics in that it has taken Katona a quarter of a century to convince economists that there can be mass changes in willingness by consumers to spend and make commitments, as events and people's perceptions of them alter their confidence in their own and their country's economic future. It seems such a straightforward proposition, such a relatively simple theory, and so crucial to dynamic economic analysis and forecasting. And it did not multiply the explanatory variables inordinately. A substantial accumulation of empirical evidence over many years shows that occasionally at crucial times there are mass changes in attitudes followed by changes in levels of consumption expenditure. The accumulated information on the national and personal events that preceded and accompanied those changes in attitudes allows the development of theory about how people see and interpret their environment, and how they learn from history as each new event impinges on a revised set of information and beliefs.

Since aggregate (average) levels of consumer optimism predict individual spending behavior better than the individual's own optimism, we clearly need a theory about the way perceptions of other people's attitudes affect our own behavior.

Ignorance

It is not merely uncertainty about the future that inhibits spending and affects its content. There is ignorance (or undertainty about the facts), and also confusion about how one uses facts to make decisions on economic choices. The field of consumer economics is full of admonitions to consumers to stop doing irrational things, meaning failing to get facts or to use them properly.

Such behavior may not be irrational, however, if information is expensive to secure, relative to the possible gains. There is a growing theoretical literature in economics about optimal information-search strategy in both purchasing and job searching, though few empirical studies of actual behavior.[4] Of course, the economic theory of a market economy shows how it can approach optimality under a set of assumptions, a crucial one being that individual actors are informed.

We have proposed a continuous telephone-interviewing and feedback system for a local community that would test the economic feasibility of such a local information service, and at the same time assess its effects on market functioning.[5] Probability samples, various adjustments for biases, and the law of large numbers should allow us to bypass any need for precise measurement of quality of service. We argue that quality is whatever leads to satisfaction, for the most part, and that knowing the fraction of the customers of each competitor who are satisfied with the quality/price is the kind of information most of us have been using anyway.

Given what I have said about the inhibiting effects of ignorance of market facts, my guess would be that the main effect of such a system would be to expand the total demand for services toward the best vendors, while encouraging the others to improve. (Many of the deficiencies may well be unknown to the management.) Better information about the quality/prices of local repair services may encourage repairs and conserve resources by postponing replacement.

Perhaps the most exciting thing about such an experiment is that it can have two alternative possible outcomes. First, the correlation between price and quality can improve so rapidly that no one would be willing to pay for the information about the remaining differences. In this case, the social benefits of information are obviously large, widely spread, and justify subsidy out of public funds. Second, the improvement may be slow, erratic, and subject to changing conditions among the vendors, so that it remains valuable to users to have the information. In that case, a local consumer information service is an economically viable system, and the design is exportable to other communities.

Confusion

We now come to the final area where economic theory needs to be supplemented both by psychological theory and by empirical research if it is to be useful; namely, how people apply the insights of economic analysis to ordinary choices, or fail to do so. There is abundant evidence that consumers lack the economic understanding and problem solving abilities to act in a way which economic theory says is optimal, given their goals. I have labeled this situation "confusion," because people are confused as to which facts they need and what to do with the facts in making decisions. The great policy debate as to the relative role of consumer information versus more consumer protection by the government hinges on whether the consumers are not just informable but also educable as to what to do with information.

For example, the payoff to finishing high school, it turns out, is the sum of a set of expected values, each the product of the payoff to an alternative future opened up by the high school diploma, times the probability that that will be the future path. Many of us don't really believe in probabilities, much less in *adding* the expected values of alternatives. And the payoff to shopping one more store turns out to depend on an estimate of price/quality variability that must be continuously adjusted for each new bit of information. Do we expect consumers to be Bayesians as well as probabilists?

There is some interesting research going on in information processing, but the most important problems of the consumer are not information overload, but lack of any cognitive structure.[6] We need empirical research here. It may be that consumers have other motives or constraints. James Duesenberry's famous statement reminds us: Economics is all about how people make decisions. Sociology is all about why they don't have any decisions to make. Indeed, social pressures, reference groups, acceptable roles, and the inevitable course of the family life cycle may dominate many decisions.

33

Katona (1975) has summarized much of what we know about the psychology of economic behavior. People are ignorant, but not dumb; they lack theory and insight, but have rules of thumb that often save them; they can be led by the media and other devices, but not very far away from what satisfies and pleases. Their behavior is for the most part meaningful to them, even though it may seem irrational by normative standards of deductive economic theory.

This may explain why studies of shopping and information-getting make consumers seem so far from optimum behavior as the economist defines it. They may be relying on information already half processed, less specific but more useful and cheaper to get. The readers of *Consumer Reports (CU)* over the years repeatedly insisted on rankings and "best buy" indications, implying that they are willing to trust *CU*'s criteria weights and save time and energy. An early study by Mueller and Katona indicated circumspect and deliberate shopping for sports shirts, and less shopping than expected for major applicances, presumably because there was more variety of style and more chance for regret with the former.

It is entirely plausible that one result of the combination of ignorance, uncertainty, and confusion is inhibition of action entirely. Some years ago a research project provided a sample of consumers with market and quality information, and another sample with exhortations to buy wisely, and then went back to see which group seemed to be buying most wisely in terms of the price/quality information made available to one group. The results were clear — the group with detailed information did not buy noticeably "better," they simply bought *more*.

It is change in behavior that matters; hence, the relevant psychological theory is that of perception and/or learning, combined with a theory of motivation. How do people perceive changes in their environment; what cognitive insights lead them to infer what they should do about it; and what do they learn from the results of their past behavior? This kind of dynamic question is hard to investigate. There is some panel study analysis (see Duncan and Hill, 1975). The author has proposed a study that will ask people how their choices affected one another as each person settled into a job, a marriage, a spouse's job, a decision about children, and a location.

The author also once proposed some research on why people do not use the logical processes the economists say they should. It was suggested that in a sequence of questions we could lead a respondent through the "proper" considerations and inferences, and then see whether he came to the expected conclusions, rejected them because of other considerations, totally refused to accept the logic, or understood everything but admitted making actual decisions much more casually.

Summary and Conclusions

When there are many complicated problems, we need a research strategy. Such a strategy combines guesses both about potential results (productivity of the research) and about the value of the conclusions. In economic behavior, it is mass dynamics that matters most to the nation, not interpersonal differences that cancel out. We also want results that bear on policy issues and may affect major government programs or policies. My own judgment is that pushing faster on the study of the effects of uncertainty and of confidence and optimism on willingness to spend and make commitments by consumers ranks first. Then would come research on the effect of improved simple information on consumer behavior and market functioning. Third, we need to find out how to educate people about economics so they can solve their own economic choice problems effectively. Fourth, we may want to know how families solve their joint decision problems, and lastly, how complex sets of wants combine with attributes of products in an uncertain world to affect people's desires.

Notes

1. This chapter is reproduced from an article by James N. Morgan entitled "Multiple Motives, Group Decisions, Uncertainty, Ignorance, and Confusion: A Realistic Economics of the Consumer Requires Some Psychology," *American Economic Review — Papers and Proceedings, 68,* 2 (May 1978), 58–63. Copyright 1978 by the American Economic Association. Reprinted with permission.

2. See Atkinson (1964); Atkinson and Feather (1966); and Atkinson and Raynor (1974).

3. For an assessment of the quantitative importance of change in family composition in accounting for the variance in change of status, see Duncan and Morgan (1977). And for a study of factors affecting changes in family composition, see Duncan and Morgan (1976). For estimates of the value of intrafamily transfers, see Baerwaldt and Morgan (1978). For attempts to clear up the conceptual confusion about social security, see Morgan (1976 and 1977).

4. For studies of deliberation in purchasing, see Katona and Mueller (1954) and Newman and Staehlin (1972). For studies of job search, see Sheppard and Belitsky (1966) and Granovetter (1974).

5. So far it is only an unfunded proposal and some pilot work. See Maynes et al. (1977).

6. Most of this work is coming out of Purdue. See Jacoby, Chestnut, and Silberman (1977); Jacoby, Olson, and Haddock (1971); and Jacoby, Szybillo, and Busato-Schach (1977).

3

Methodological Issues

THE MAJOR FEATURE of the method used in behavioral economics has already been pointed out at the beginning of Chapter 1. Behavioral economics is an inductive science that starts with observations of one-time events or developments and proceeds gradually to generalizations derived from repeated observations made under different circumstances. In contrast, classical economics begins with broad generalizations about human nature from which it deduces consequences for the market place and tests them by relaxing the original assumptions so that they conform with reality.

This difference will not be discussed in this chapter. Today few will dispute that both deductive and inductive methods have their place in scientific inquiry. Moreover, assumptions and hypotheses always guide the selective and systematic observations undertaken, and no scientific endeavor starts out with haphazard observations. What is in question is the source of the hypotheses used. Therefore, the broad methodological issues to be discussed in this chapter concern the role of psychological hypotheses in economic research and the question of realism of the assumptions made. We shall ask first why interdisciplinary research is necessary and then turn to a discussion of the role of realism in selecting assumptions. Both problems have frequently been misunderstood. The emphasis of Morgan on realistic economics expressed in the title of his essay reproduced in Chapter 2 of this book calls for further discussion.

Why Is Interdisciplinary Research Necessary?

Interdisciplinary research is necessary because some major problems of many sciences, including economics, fall into more than one traditional discipline. This statement is correct but not complete. Economists, for at least one hundred years, have been aware of the cross-disciplinary nature of some economic problems but have, for the most part, responded by excluding other disciplines, most notably psychology, from economics. We shall quote just one leading economist, Joseph Schumpeter, who, in a book written early in his career on the essence of economics, argued that it was not necessary and would be methodologically mistaken for economists to deal with "human conduct" and "the motives of human conduct." He wrote about the study of human conduct that "For the economic *results* it is irrelevant and it can never be the task of the economist to go into these matters."[1]

Schumpeter's argument is twofold. One aspect is a matter of definition. Economics is defined as an analysis of economic results; it is considered to deal not with the behavior of people but with the results of their behavior and the behavior of the markets. While it is futile to argue over definitions, the second aspect of Schumpteter's thesis, the assertion that the motives of human conduct are irrelevant for the economic results, may be contradicted by empirical findings.

Let us first state that although many economic theorists as well as econometricians still adhere to the same doctrine as Schumpeter, there are some leading economic theorists today who uphold the opposite view. James Tobin, when asked to contribute an essay on psychology and economics to Sigmund Koch's opus *Psychology: A Study of a Science*, chose to write a supplement to George Katona's article in Volume 6 of that series, from which the first and last sentences are as follows:

> Recent developments in economic theory have emphasized the dependence of economics on assumptions regarding the motivations of economic behavior.
> The relationship of economic behavior to personality attributes is not only a subject of interest in itself; it is also essential for correct interpretation of observed relations among economic magnitudes (Tobin and Dolbear, 1963, p. 677 and 682).

40

Empirical findings about the role of such antecedents of human behavior as motives, attitudes, and expectations that influence and alter the economic results have been presented in the first of the essays in the present volume and will be discussed in later essays as well. Of special interest at this point is the second quotation from Tobin's essay, which could be interpreted, probably incorrectly, as calling for a consideration of the manifold differences in personality characteristics among individuals. It is important to ask the following questions: Does economics require a consideration of the multitude of personality differences among businessmen and consumers? Is economics unrealistic because it puts all people in the same box, that is, because it analyzes the behavior of what is called the representative firm and disregards individual differences?

Tobin begins his discussion of personality by accepting the hypothesis underlying many years of studies by the Survey Research Center according to which "The attitudes of optimism or pessimism are relevant to the short-term outlook for consumer spending" (1963, p. 682). But he argues that attitudes cannot help very much for the solution of long-term problems, for which task "the relationship of economic behavior — e.g., spending and saving — to more fundamental and permanent dimensions of personality" would have to be explored. He refers to Katona's studies conducted in the 1950s and 1960s indicating that families with substantial liquid assets added to their assets (saved) more than families with small liquid assets, irrespective of income levels. These findings contradicted a widely accepted thesis of economic theory assuming that those who have little have greater needs and therefore ought to save more than those who have much. But the findings confirmed two psychological principles. The first relates to the lasting influence of thrifty dispositions (a personality type) and of long-established habits of saving, which in most cases are responsible for the holdings of families with substantial liquid assets. The second principle is the one already cited in Chapter 1 that accomplishment raises people's levels of aspiration. Accomplishment in this case consists of having been able to accumulate substantial liquid assets, in which case, except under extreme conditions and in the absence of disappointments, people want still more rather than feel satiated. Personality characteristics do matter. In order to explain differences in the rate of saving in different countries, it is useful to find out whether the proportion of people with thrifty dispositions and established habits of saving and borrowing is larger or smaller in one or the other country. But economists concerned with differences in the rate of saving need study only the distribution of the dispositions and habits in the entire country rather than any individual differences.

The two tendencies expressed in the two hypotheses above operate together. Rising aspirations for higher and higher assets — the amounts of savings and reserve funds once desired appearing insufficient after they have been reached — reinforce saving habits. Tobin separates the two tendencies and draws a broad conclusion for economic policy. If saving much were mainly motivated by rising aspirations, then, Tobin argues, "it would be foolish to worry about possible inflationary effects of high liquidity" (1963).

What is disregarded here is the basic hypothesis governing studies in behavioral economics, namely, the principle of learning. Because human beings are capable of learning, their response to the same stimulus may differ at a later time from what it was earlier. Attitudes, expectations, and aspirations also may change as the result of learning. The 1950s and 1960s were times of rising aspirations; in the 1970s aspirations were scaled down. The impact of rapid inflation on the value of accumulated bank deposits — even though softened by the receipt of high interest — made for disappointment and uncertainty among some people. Even in 1979 the great majority of Americans considered saving, including saving in banks, a "good thing" and desired larger liquid assets. But these general attitudes did not hinder them from purchasing houses, cars, and other durable goods in large quantities even before they were urgently needed, in order to acquire them before their prices went up further and to use their liquid assets for down payments and partial payments in addition to incurring mortgage and installment debt. "High liquidity" of American families was not worrisome in the 1950s and 1960s but did become worrisome in the 1970s because in the meantime the American people had acquired new experiences, opinions, and insights about inflation.

Change matters most, and in this respect behavioral economics follows traditional economics. One of the great achievements of nineteenth century economics was the introduction of marginal analysis. Marginalism focuses attention on effects of changes in conditions. It assumes that every economic decision is taken for the sake of the difference it will make and investigates the question, what difference would the change make. Even though in many instances this theoretical position led to an extreme definition of the economic man — assuming that he always tries to maximize utilities — the basic lesson of marginalism should not be disregarded.

The interdisciplinary approach is useful for the purpose of understanding and predicting both short and long-term economic trends. To support this statement it may suffice to point to Chapter 1's discussion of the experience with the Index of Consumer Sentiment on the one hand and of the new economic era in the 1970s on the other.

As a footnote to the preceding discussion, a few words may be needed about how interdisciplinary research is conducted. It is possible for even a single researcher working alone to adopt an interdisciplinary orientation. Each of our disciplines is so complex and varied today that no one can become a true expert in all segments of one discipline. A researcher may specialize in several economic subdisciplines or, alternatively, in one or two economic and one or two psychological or sociological subdisciplines. Large-scale research projects are conducted by a team of several researchers who may be recruited from two or more disciplines. Working together on a problem, they may utilize lines of thought foreign to their original discipline and thereby form an inter-disciplinary team. Usually, in the experience of the Survey Research Center, team members who originally came from, say, economics and others who came from, say, psychology participated in the studies of all problems, lost their identification with their original discipline and became problem-oriented rather than discipline-oriented. The use of the sample interview survey, the most important tool of behavioral economics, facilitates problem orientation. In these surveys it is possible to collect financial and attitudinal data from the same individuals and relate them to one another.

Realism in Economics[2]

In his important methodological essay, Milton Friedman (1959) raised the question: "Can an hypothesis be tested by the realism of its assumptions?" Obviously, the answer to this question is "No." Derivations from hypotheses or consequences of hypotheses, rather than their assumptions, are tested by confronting them with data from the real world. The purpose of the test is to find out whether the two conform and whether the hypothesis serves to advance knowledge about reality.

Scientific knowledge has two sources: Measurement of what is, one source, is interlaced with the contribution of the scientist, the other source. The scientist constructs assumptions and hypotheses which are abstract and tentative. In addition to determining what to observe, the hypotheses serve the purpose of creating order among the multitude of observations. Hypotheses may be derived from casual observation or from alleged general principles and from imagination. They represent the creative or intuitive contributions of the scholar, arrived at through reorganizing and restructuring the problem in such a way that something new emerges from

44

familiar material. Jacob Bronowski presented the thesis beautifully in his essay on *Science and Human Values* (1956, also 1978). He argues that science shares a common origin with art in the wellspring of imagination and that neither art nor science copies nature. Science, Bronowski says, is a creation because scientific activity is not a passive state of recognition but an active relation between the observer and his world. Therefore, we may conclude, there is nothing methodologically wrong in starting out with such unrealistic assumptions as complete information, complete mobility, or perfect competition.

But Friedman, by raising the question quoted above and scornfully rejecting an affirmative answer to the question, has not addressed himself to the fundamental difference between traditional and realistic economics. It is this: Traditional economic theory has not proved to be a complete success, many of its implications and predictions having not proved to be correct. One possible way of attempting to improve traditional theory of economic behavior is to introduce new assumptions and hypotheses. Behavioral economists did just this and chose to derive their new realistic hypotheses from psychological and sociological theory. They focused attention on such psychological antecedents of economic behavior as attitudes, expectations, and motives.

The basic theoretical principle of which behavioral economics makes use is the denial of a one-to-one correspondence between stimuli and responses and the acknowledgment of the influence of intervening variables. Behavior is a function of both the person and the environment. Fixed and unchangeable relations between stimuli or precipitating circumstances and responses or behavior are rare exceptions. The simple model of reflex action is not valid in matters involving higher mental activity, and thus it is not valid in economic behavior. Stimuli, be they personal experiences or information received, do not fully determine the response by the economic actor. Even what we hear, see, or experience is colored by our attitudes and motives, and also by socio-cultural norms and habits as well as by group belonging. All these variables intervene between stimuli and responses and, occasionally, powerfully influence our responses. As we said before, we may respond to the same stimuli the second time differently from the first time because new attitudes may have developed in the meantime that influence the response in a different way. These assumptions are more realistic than those of traditional theory. But support for the assumptions can be derived only from analyzing the consequences of the assumptions.

Although there exist theories that integrate a set of hypotheses and observations at an early stage of scientific inquiry, they are not common in science. Usually, first, low-level hypotheses are tested through the process of systematic observations characterising empirical research. Such tests hardly ever result in confirmation of a hypothesis and not often in its rejection. What one usually learns from tests is how to improve, revise, or reformulate the hypothesis and then testing must be taken up again. Scientific inquiry consists of a neverending process of hypothesis, test of hypothesis through controlled and replicable observation, reformulation and revision of hypothesis, more tests, and so on. Such procedures result in empirically validated generalizations, which represent the proximate aim of scientific research.

The elegant simplicity of traditional economic theory represents one of its great assets. Must it be destroyed by the introduction of psychological variables and thus an increase in the number of variables to be considered? We must remember the last two words in the classical law of parsimony: *Entia non sunt multiplicanda praeter necessitatem*. We may ask whether such formulations as "Under conditions a_1, b_1, c_1, the consequence of X (say, of a price reduction) is likely to be Y_1 (say, larger sales) while, under conditions a_2, b_2, c_2, it is likely to be Y_2 (smaller sales)" are less elegant than the traditional law of supply and demand. Or suppose research validates a generalization such as: "Under conditions a_1, b_1, c_1 (e.g., prosperous times, large reserves, optimistic attitudes), business firms strive for longer-range objectives than under conditions a_2, b_2, c_2." Would such a generalization constitute introducing unnecessary complexities into the principle of profit maximization?

Nothing is more practical than good theory, according to Kurt Lewin. Bronowski emphasized that there need not be deep boundaries between knowledge and its use. The author's attempts during the past 30 years to make predictions of economic trends from systematic measurement of changes in consumer attitudes and expectations have often been called applied psychology, or applied economics. But survey research serves a purpose beyond that of describing reality and even predicting reality. By deriving predictions from hypotheses and theories we make way for the most powerful of scientific tests. This is the means whereby we let nature decide how our hypotheses need to be revised. To be sure, since reality is complex our tests are seldom if ever pure. Nevertheless, scholars must dare to predict, and progress may be achieved through both correct and incorrect predictions. Prediction is also a practical necessity. Much of behavior, and of economic behavior in particular, is oriented toward the future. Our image of the future determines our actions. This image is derived from past experience, and yet the statement that the past governs the future is correct only in a certain sense. History does not repeat itself. We do not always do what we have done before in similar circumstances, and extrapolation is not a generally valid guide to the future. Hypotheses and theories, developed in the past, provide the best predictions and at the same time shape our image of the future.

Theory construction is part of the process of testing and revising hypotheses. Theories represent an integration of different hypotheses relating to different aspects of reality.

47

The distant goal to which behavioral economics contributes is a theory of social behavior rather than economic behavior. Integrated principles of motivation, group membership, learning, and decision making must be developed in all areas of human activity, including behavior toward material resources.

Notes

1. Joseph Schumpeter (1908, p. 542). The sentence is quoted as translated by Fritz Machlup (1978, p. 465).

2. Some arguments incorporated in this section have been presented earlier in the author's Comment included in a Social Science Research Council pamphlet (Bowen, 1955, p. 42 ff.) and in Katona (1960, p. 262 ff.).

4

Macro and Micro Uncertainty

For a long time uncertainty has been a topic of great interest to economists.[1] Economic theorists, recognizing that the most important business decisions are future-oriented and that the future is uncertain, developed probability models about how businessmen cope with uncertainty. This author, in his studies of the psychological determinants of economic processes, approached the problem of uncertainty from a different angle. In his endeavors to forecast economic trends through collecting survey data on changes in attitudes and expectations, he was impressed by the fact that the survey approach to forecasting was successful on the aggregate or macro level, while on the micro level it was impossible or very difficult to provide evidence for the influence of the attitudes of individuals on their subsequent actions. The Index of Consumer Sentiment represents a macro measure reflecting the changes in the attitudes and expectations of all Americans. When the Index was contrasted with another macro measure reflecting the changes in the economic activities in the entire country (e.g., changes in automobile sales or in the Gross National Product), it was found that the Index declined substantially prior to the onset of every recession during the last 25 years, and it advanced prior to the beginning of periods of economic recovery (see Chart 1, Chapter 1). In contrast, such actions of individuals as their major expenditures or additions to savings could not be predicted by the changes in their attitudes and expectations.

Thus, some consequences of macropsychological findings (e.g., change in the attitudes of the American people) and micropsychological findings (e.g., changes in the attitudes of individuals) were found to be different. This problem is

51

studied by analyzing uncertainty among all Americans as well as among some individual Americans.

In economics the distinction between macro- and micro-processes is well established, and it is well known that there are macroregularities that do not apply on the micro level. Perhaps the best known among these is that investment and saving must be equal for the economy as a whole but that the two differ for practically all individual persons and firms. Psychology is overwhelmingly micro because it is only the individual who reacts, learns, thinks, and has emotions. Social psychology also analyzes mostly how individual behavior is influenced by belonging to groups, although group norms and social forces are occasionally discussed. Does macropsychology therefore belong in sociology, or is it something hazy and unnecessary?

The proposition that psychologists ought to be involved in the study of macroprocesses is developed below by studying specific examples of economic behavior. The study and measurement of uncertainty are used to clarify the meaning of macropsychology.

In the fall of 1977, a news magazine featured the following statement: "A pervasive sense of uncertainty grips businessmen and investors." What is meant by this journalistic observation? Perhaps simply that there were in 1977 very many businessmen and investors who felt uncertain about forthcoming economic trends. Alternatively, what was meant may have been that uncertainty was "in the air," so most if not all businessmen and investors were affected by it.

In the past, psychologists have used the term *uncertainty* primarily to mean a psychological state of individuals. More recently the term has also been used to refer (for instance, in information theory) to characteristics of stimuli in a sense closely related to ambiguity. Insufficiency of clues, whether in perception or in a detective story, may create uncertainty so that additional stimuli or clues are needed to provide clarity. In this sense, the uncertainty prevailing in the economy may be identified with insufficient information or conflicting signals about forthcoming trends. Uncertainty in the sense of a puzzling situation in which contradictory outcomes are possible may also be viewed as an early and transitional phase of the problem-solving process. When a problem is solved or when full understanding is achieved in a learning situation, uncertainty is dispelled.

The economic literature on uncertainty is so voluminous that only brief references can be included here. Econometricians have tended to replace uncertain expectations with "certainty equivalents." The practice of disregarding uncertainty may have been based on John Maynard Keynes's (1936) proposition that "it would be foolish in forming one's expectations to attach great weight to matters which are very uncertain" (p. 148). This may be justified if uncertainty means that the probability assigned to an expectation is very low. Uncertainty, however, may also mean great concern with future contingencies, fear of adverse developments, and lack of confidence, which should not be neglected.

A major task at hand is the measurement of uncertainty, so as to clarify its meaning and also to confirm or reject the journalistic notion about uncertainty being pervasive in 1977. The author's first attempt to measure uncertainty was stimulated by Paul Lazarsfeld, who, in studies of the panel method, distinguished between individual respondents answering the same question at different times in the same way or in a different way (turnover). He wrote, "If the turnover is large, it indicates that the opinion or behavior is unstable. We know that people feel uncertain (Lazarsfeld, Berelson, and Gaudet, 1948, p. x).

In a paper published 20 years ago (Katona, 1958), the author has called attention to the fact that change of response from a first to a second interview might be caused by the acquisition of new information rather than by uncertainty about the answer. Distinguishing between the two was possible by contrasting the individual or micro measure of "proportion of changers" with an aggregate or trend measure indicating the extent of change from the first to the second interview. When the answers of the entire sample, representing all Americans, revealed that optimism had been growing or declining substantially, a large proportion of changers appeared to indicate a change in attitudes resulting from new information. Alternatively, the changers may be divided into two groups, those who moved in the same direction as the aggregate change and those who "swam against the current." This is done in Table 1. We see there that in 1955, for instance, the number of changers was fairly high but indicated a sizable trend (toward optimism) that occurred at that time. In 1976, on the other hand, a substantially greater proportion of changers (and a smaller proportion of consistent answers) was obtained, with changes in both directions being about equal. (Thirty-six percent of the sample shifted from pessimistic to optimistic and 28 percent from optimistic to pessimistic answers.) A large proportion of those swimming against the current — as in 1976 and, to a lesser extent, in 1971 and 1977 — points toward a great volatility of response (see Katona and Strumpel, 1978, chap. 4). Yet it is far from assured that volatility is identical with uncertainty. Therefore, the search for other measures of uncertainty has continued.

A volatility measure based on the extent of changes in the Index of Consumer Sentiment and therefore on changes in the aggregate response of the entire sample was used next. As is shown in Chart 2, suggested by Richard Curtin, this measure indicates little volatility from 1965 to 1972 and great volatility from 1972 to 1978. Again, the observed volatility may be interpreted in different ways; it may or may not reflect uncertainty.

Therefore, a third measure was constructed, based on the dispersion of responses. At a time when almost everybody in a representative sample expresses optimistic expectations, or almost everybody expresses pessimistic expectations, we may say that the people are optimistic or pessimistic. On the other

TABLE 1

Measures of Volatility on the Micro Level
in Two Consecutive Interviews

| Date of 2nd interview | Percent consistent | Percent of changers | |
		Trend	Swimming against current
June 1955	56	30	14
September 1964	69	17	14
September 1971	57	23	20
October 1973	57	27	16
May 1975	47	37	16
October 1976	36	36	28
May 1977	57	23	19
September 1977	58	24	18

Note. Two interviews were conducted with identical respondents at 6-month intervals. The answers to three questions — personal financial expectations during the next year, and general economic outlook for the next year and for the next five years — were averaged. The three questions are parts of the Index of Consumer Sentiment. The sample sizes were between 600 and 1,600.

hand, when a substantial proportion is optimistic and a similar substantial proportion is pessimistic, the people as a whole may be viewed as uncertain in their expectations about future developments. Thus, the smaller the difference between those expecting good or better times and those expecting bad or worse times, the greater the uncertainty on the aggregate or macro level. This measure, constructed irrespective of whether optimists or pessimists were more frequent (i.e., by disregarding signs), is shown in Chart 3. It indicates that growing optimism dispelled uncertainty (as in 1965) and so did growing pessimism (as in 1974). The chart shows that from 1969 to 1977 uncertainty was substantially greater than in the preceding 20 years. In spite of the high level of uncertainty in 1957 — prior to the 1958 recession — and the low level

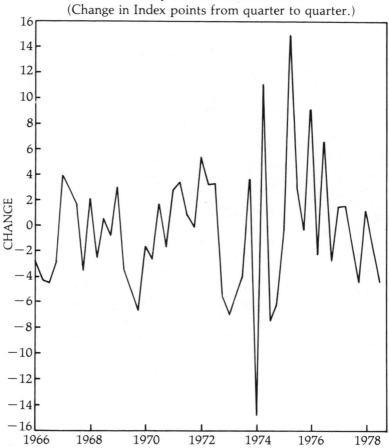

CHART 2
Volatility of Consumer Sentiment
(Change in Index points from quarter to quarter.)

of uncertainty in 1974 during the deepest postwar recession — there were differences between the earlier decades and the 1970s. In most of the 1970s the uncertainty index registered 150 or more, while in the 1960s the average reading was close to 100.

The question of how to measure uncertainty is rather complex. So are the consequences of uncertainty. Zajonc and Burnstein (1961) concluded from an experimental study that "the likelihood of cognitive changes increases with increasing uncertainty" (p. 115). This conclusion is in accord with our linking uncertainty with the volatility and instability of attitudes and behavior. Weighty arguments have also been marshalled for another consequence of uncertainty: "When in doubt, do nothing," goes an old adage. Economists frequently argue that uncertainty retards or even inhibits spending and investing because people feeling uncertain about the future tend to abstain from committing large funds. The two assumptions about the consequences of uncertainty are not necessarily contradictory, yet they call for further investigation for which, probably, a study of economic behavior may be most suitable.

To clarify the meaning of macro data in contrast with micro data, a comparison of the methods used in Table 1 and Chart 3 may be helpful. Though Table 1 indicates that it is possible to measure the extent of the uncertainty and volatility of attitudes of individuals, Chart 3 does not reflect individual attitudes or behavior. Data obtained from a large number of people are characterized in Chart 3 either by uniformity, by concensus and fit in a normal curve, or by dispersion, divergence, and fit in a U curve. The macropsychological data appear to add something to the usual micropsychological data.

What must be added to these considerations is a plea for further research. We need to know much more than we do both about micro uncertainty — individuals displaying uncertainty — and about macro uncertainty — high frequency of un-

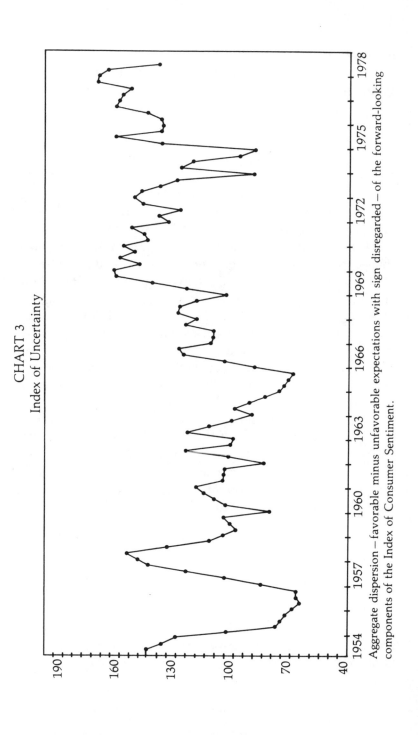

CHART 3
Index of Uncertainty

Aggregate dispersion – favorable minus unfavorable expectations with sign disregarded – of the forward-looking components of the Index of Consumer Sentiment.

certainty among the members of a given universe, for instance, all Americans. How uncertainty spreads among people and how people cope with it represent crucial problems that may be studied by analyzing economic attitudes and various forms of economic behavior. For the present, we shall restrict our discussion to advancing the following hypothesis about coping with uncertainty:

Belief and trust in continuity and stability are common. Uncertainty of the future is disregarded unless strong motivational forces intervene. Confusion and disorientation then lead to either doing nothing, or to shifting from one response to the opposite one and back again (vacillation and volatility).

An important question arises beyond that of the ways of responding to or coping with uncertainty. Under which conditions are we aware of uncertainty and confronted with the necessity to choose and make genuine decisions?

Psychological studies of decision making often presuppose the presence of definite expectations about the future. For instance, experiments carried out by Tversky and Kahneman and reported in several articles asked subjects questions such as whether they preferred a "25 percent change to gain $300" or a "20 percent change to gain $400." These kinds of alternatives, perhaps present in some cases of gambling, are not typical of economic behavior. Neither businessmen nor investors in stocks know in advance the exact probabilities of chance or the specific amounts of expected gain. Their expectations are typically vague and uncertain. True, it was found that expecting to make either a gain or a loss was infrequent; but when people expected to make a gain, they were highly uncertain about its extent and its probability. The elimination of uncertainty through "certainty equivalents," represented by assuming knowledge of the probability of future events, contributes little to an understanding of either the psychological or the economic processes as they usually occur.

Studies of decision making must go beyond studies of

choice between exact probabilities given. A similar require-
ment confronts the usual experiments in problem solving.
When subjects are presented with problems, as is done in
practically all experiments, an important phase of problem
solving is eliminated from the study: recognizing that there is
a problem. We tend to just go on and do what we did before,
or do nothing, rather than perceiving that a problem and a
choice exist. Uncertainty in the sense of hesitation and the
notion that we better "stop and look" before we act are not
always present. The circumstances under which awareness of
uncertainty arises must be studied.

In closing, we return to the problem of the consequences of
attitudes on the macro and the micro levels and the problem
of predicting aggregate rather than individual behavior.
Optimistic or pessimistic attitudes of individuals may change
quickly and are affected by a great variety of factors. On the
other hand, optimism and pessimism or uncertainty of the
masses tend to change slowly and gradually and are subject
to little noise. The prediction of macro behavior is made possible by its relatively steady and enduring nature.

Many factors cancel out when the attitudes and behavior
of very large groups are compared, notably differences in
mood and the age of the respondent. An individual's response
may be subject to temporary changes in his mood, favorable
or unfavorable, that happen to be influential at the time of
questioning. Furthermore, changes in the attitudes and
behavior of individuals may occur at different points in time.
Some individuals may become optimistic in their economic
outlook or uncertain about their prospects very early and
others rather late in the business cycle; the occurrence of attitude change and of purchases of durable goods may not coin-
cide with their measurement. In studying attitudes and
actions, the timing of measurement presents much smaller
problems among masses of people than among few people or
individuals.

Attitudes and expectations such as optimism or pessimism,

confidence or uncertainty, spread like a contagious disease. The mass media transmit and emphasize good as well as bad news rather uniformly and the news is reinforced by word of mouth over extensive periods. The prediction of macrobehavior is facilitated by the continuation of trends in the American people's attitudes and purchases over several months. A statement based on the measurement of macro attitudes, such as "Today the American people are characterized by a high degree of uncertainty," is meaningful and has specific consequences. In the final chapter we discuss how in 1979 the prevailing uncertainty, pessimism, and absence of confidence made the fight against inflation very difficult.

Notes

1. Portions of this chapter are reproduced from the article, "Toward a Macropsychology," *American Psychologist, 34*, 2 (February 1979), 118–126. Copyright 1979 by the American Psychological Association. Reprinted by permission. Much of this chapter will also appear in *Uncertainty*, a book edited by Seymour Fiddle, to be published by Praeger Publishers, New York.

5

A Summer of Discontent

DISCONTENT WAS A MAJOR FEATURE of the economic situation in the summer of 1979. Emphasis on this prevailing psychological climate focuses attention on a significant aspect of economic trends in the late seventies. It is important to know how psychological factors, beyond the impact of economic-financial developments and the actions of OPEC, have contributed to America's economic problems. This was hinted at, rather than demonstrated, by President Carter when, in his nationwide television address of July 1979, he placed the crisis of confidence in the center of his discussion of inflation and the oil crisis.

Past Trends

In the midst of our concern about two-digit inflation, recession, and the energy problem, we may well turn the clock back 25 years and note how the American economy looked at that time. Barbara Ward, a well-known student of the world's economic and political developments and a leading member of the *London Economist*'s editorial board, in her book *Faith and Freedom* (1954), contrasted the stability and progress of the 100 years before 1914 with the disturbances of the following 35 years that witnessed two world wars and the worldwide depression of the 1930s. Yet, her analysis of the American economy allowed her to look forward to the future with great optimism. American hegemony, political as well as economic, would in her opinion guarantee prosperity and progress all over the globe. She pointed to the existence of a strong currency, the dollar, which would not be affected by disturbances in the rest of the world. She argued that the dollar shortage prevailing in the 1950s in Europe and in the underdeveloped countries would be overcome by foreign aid and by American development of natural resources in Africa, Asia, and South America. Fluctuations in the domestic American economy would cease to be troublesome as booms and busts would be levelled off by tax increases or cuts as well as by public works, particularly for housing and slum clearance.

Barbara Ward's predictions were true — for about ten years. To be sure, the American economy suffered a severe recession in 1958. Yet the weakness of the dollar was not apparent until 1965. In the next few years, when the United States indulged in financing the war in Vietnam through deficit spending, inflation became somewhat more pronounced. A recession in 1970 was fairly short, and in February 1971 President Nixon began his *Economic Report* by speaking of a recovery "leading to a new steadiness of expansion in the years beyond." But just a few months later the President responded to inflation and the weakness of the dollar by introducing general price and wage controls and suspending the convertibility of the dollar into gold (pegged from 1934 to 1971 at $35 an ounce).

What has happened since 1971 hardly needs to be recalled in detail. The dollar became the weak currency of the world, losing 27 percent of its value between early 1971 and late 1978 (calculated on the basis of multilateral trade-weighted averages; the German mark doubled its value in dollars during this period and gold rose to more than $200 an ounce).[1] Inflation accelerated greatly, with retail prices advancing by 75 percent during those eight years. Two-digit inflation in 1974 coincided with the deepest postwar recession recorded. Toward the end of that recession, unemployment was as high as 9 percent. The substantial recovery following the recession remained spotty, with business investment in capital goods lagging behind. By 1978, the onset of a new recession threatened.

Some reasons for the radical change in the international

position of the dollar are well known. Prosperous Americans greatly increased their purchases of foreign goods. But in 1971, the first year of the currency crisis, the trade deficit was less than three billion dollars. Long-term investments by American industries abroad rose to such an extent that Servan-Schreiber described American subsidiaries in Europe as the second greatest industrial power in the world (industry in the U.S. being the first). Yet much more important than these changes were the withdrawals of short-term funds, which in the 1950s and 1960s sought refuge and safety in the United States. As early as 1971, the official tabulation of the balance of payment transactions listed "errors and un-recorded transactions" at minus 11 billion dollars. What was unrecorded were movements of liquid funds. The amount of unregulated funds searching for a safe place at that time was very high; Eurodollars were estimated at more than 100 billion dollars a few years later, and these funds were increased substantially by Petrodollars after 1974. The currency in which investors sought refuge for these funds was, and still is, determined more by levels of trust and confidence rather than by purely economic considerations.

At that time, Americans as well had little confidence in their economy. The Index of Consumer Sentiment of the Survey Research Center fell from its peak of over 90 in the fall of 1972 to 72 in the fall of 1973, prior to the oil embargo. The decline in confidence stemmed from rapid increases in food prices and in overall inflation as well as from dwindling trust in the government. As Chart 4 shows, the deterioration in opinions about the government's economic policy corresponded to the decline in consumer expectations. A "friend-ly" critic of the predictive value of consumer expectations told the author in 1974, "You are lucky; your 1973 prediction of a forthcoming recession proved correct because shortly after you made your prediction something happened that you did not foresee, namely, the oil embargo." Yet we may ask: If the subsequent OPEC action had not occurred, would the deteri-

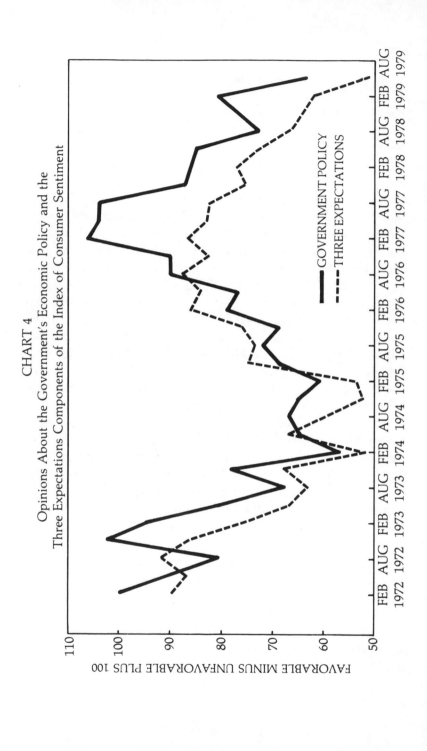

CHART 4

Opinions About the Government's Economic Policy and the
Three Expectations Components of the Index of Consumer Sentiment

Chart 4 is based on the following questions asked by the Institute for Social Research's Survey Research Center in its quarterly surveys:

Government policy: "As to the economic policy of the government — I mean steps taken to fight inflation or unemployment — would you say the government is doing a good job, only fair, or a poor job?"

Three expectations: "Looking ahead — do you think that a year from now you (and your family living there) will be better off financially, or worse off, or just about the same as now?"

"Now turning to business conditions in the country as a whole — do you think that during the next 12 months we'll have good times financially or bad times, or what?"

"Looking ahead, which would you say is more likely — that in the country as a whole we'll have continuous good times during the next 5 years or so, or that we will have periods of widespread unemployment or depression or what?"

oration of consumer sentiment have had no significant impact? Past experience regarding the influence on cyclical trends of people's willingness to buy contradicts the notion that the recession of 1973–75 was caused by OPEC alone.

Both consumer optimism and confidence in the government revived in 1975–76 — primarily during a short "Carter honeymoon" following his election. Large purchases of automobiles and one-family houses led the ensuing recovery. They were, however, motivated not just by optimism. Beginning in 1977 a buy-in-advance psychology developed as the result of people trying to beat inflation. Survey data revealed that in 1978 more than one-third of those who purchased cars and houses did so before they really needed them because they feared that later they would be priced out of the market. Consumers' willingness to borrow from the future added fuel to inflation.

In the fall of 1977 consumer sentiment once again began to deteriorate, and by late 1978 the Index and especially its expectational components (see Chart 4) declined so greatly that a weakening of consumers' willingness to buy and a new recession were clearly indicated. Survey research also pointed toward the reasons for consumers' disappointment and disenchantment. Accelerating inflation, with its impact on the real purchasing power of an evergrowing proportion of families, and distrust in the government's ability to slow down inflation and improve business conditions were the major explanations for the pessimistic outlook. But the recession was postponed because buying in advance stimulated consumer demand. Then, in 1979, there came a sharp increase in crude oil prices by OPEC and shortages of gasoline. Both the Index of Consumer Sentiment and confidence in the government continued to deteriorate sharply. Again, the Survey Research Center may have been called "lucky" for the accuracy of its forewarning. But can the economic slowdown of 1979 be said to have been caused by OPEC when it was clearly indicated by an earlier sharp deterioration of the psychological climate?

Inflation in 1979

Psychological factors contributed greatly to the acceleration of inflation both in 1978 and 1979. Prior to the summer of 1979 the federal government's deficit was curtailed, the money supply ceased to advance, interest rates were raised, the international position of the dollar improved, and price and wage guidelines were introduced and showed some impact. But improvement in the objective conditions enhancing inflation did not slow down the upward movement of prices, even in areas other than energy and food. What contributed strongly to the general inflation in 1978-79 was the behavior of the people. Consumers, rather than resisting price advances by reducing their purchases of those goods with the greatest price increases, resorted to advance buying in fear of further price advances. Business firms had no fear that higher prices would lower sales and therefore did not hesitate to transmit promptly all cost increases to their customers. Even anticipatory pricing — that is, setting prices so as to compensate not only for past increases in costs but for expected future increases as well — became a common business practice. The belief that prices would go up and up and that nothing could be done to arrest inflation served to drive prices up. Over many years as the Survey Research Center questioned representative samples of Americans about the extent of price increases they expected during the following twelve months, the answers received lagged behind actual recent price increases. Not so in 1978-79.

How do we know that consumers actually bought in advance of need? There were, of course, casual observations reported by newspapers, especially at a late date when the rapid increase in house prices called for comment. For more than 25 years the Survey Research Center has included a question in its periodic attitude surveys asking, "Do you think the next twelve months or so will be a good time or a bad time to buy a car." (Two additional questions have asked the same about one-family houses and major household goods such as refrigerators, TV sets, stoves, etc.) In 1977 the responses to all three questions improved greatly — the proportion of "good time" answers exceeded the proportion of "bad time" answers to a larger extent than earlier. In 1978 and 1979 the answers remained very favorable at a time when all other expectations worsened substantially.

Each of the three questions on "good or bad time to buy" has always been supplemented by the nondirective probe, "Why do you say so?" Over two decades the most frequent reasons for the opinion "It is a good time to buy" were that prices were low and satisfactory or that good buys were available, while the "bad time" responses were predominantly explained by saying that prices were too high. But beginning in 1977 these reasons were mentioned only rarely. A new type of answer became frequent: "Prices are going up, they won't come down; one has to buy before they get any higher." Or as one respondent put it: "If we don't buy a house today, we will never be able to buy one." It can be seen from Chart 5 that this type of spontaneous explanation was given by only 10 percent of respondents in 1975 (by still fewer in earlier years), by about 20 percent in 1976, and by 40 percent in 1978. Among respondents who actually purchased a house or car, the proportion giving this answer was often higher than among all upper-income people. As mentioned before, it appears from an analysis of these data that in 1977–78 the purchases of at least one-third of all one-family houses and new cars were motivated by fear of further inflation rather than by immediate needs or wants.

Up to the mid-1970s all economic attitudes and expectations were found to either improve or to deteriorate together. Between 1974 and 1980, however, many expectations wors-

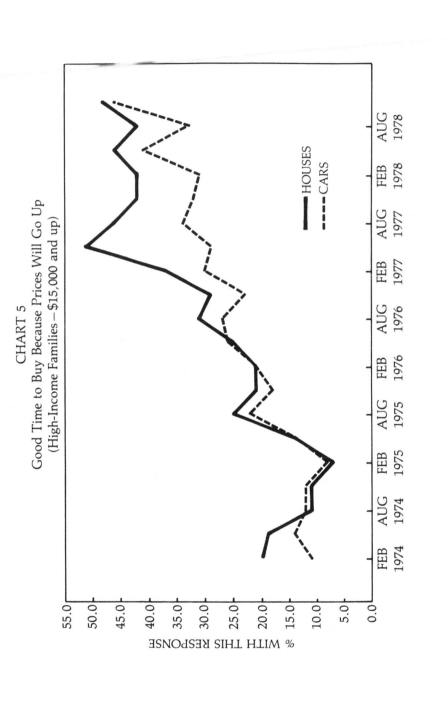

CHART 5
Good Time to Buy Because Prices Will Go Up
(High-Income Families—$15,000 and up)

ened greatly, while some other attitudes improved. Among the former were opinions about the future trend of the economy; among the latter were expressions of people's willingness to spend — although the motivation was fear of inflation.

In an extensive study of inflation conducted in July and August 1979, the Survey Research Center used a question in which respondents were asked specifically whether one should buy houses and durable goods "even before they are really needed."

> *Question:* How about large purchases such as a house, car, household appliances, and furniture. Should people buy these things nowadays even before they are really needed?
> *Responses:* Should buy, 19%; Should not buy, 71% (Depends 7%, Don't know 3%, N=2110.)

There is a widely accepted stereotype that everything we buy we do need. Nevertheless, undeterred by the phrase "buy even before they are really needed," every fifth respondent expressed approval of trying to beat inflation by advance buying. We should keep in mind that the data from the summer of 1979 refer to all Americans, not just to buyers of houses and durables, and were collected after the start of the economic slowdown.

Similar data were obtained between 1974 and 1979 by repeatedly asking a question in which two alternatives were presented: "When prices go up, some people buy things they need before prices go up even further, while others react by trying to cut down their spending because they are worried about making ends meet; what do you do when prices go up?" During those years 12 to 19 percent reported buying in advance and 39 to 66 percent said they tried to cut down spending. (Most others said that they did what they had always done, or that they only bought things when they needed them.)

The strength and extent of inflationary psychology as it developed in 1979 should not be overestimated. Many old

74

stereotypes which, it may be argued, should no longer be valid in times of rapid inflation, remained unshaken. Americans overwhelmingly maintained the old notion that in times of inflation it is necessary to economize, to shop around more carefully than in the past, and to save.

Responses to several questions asked during the summer of 1979 about what it was best to do in a time of rapid inflation are reproduced below.[2]

Question: Have you cut down on buying things which have had large price increases?
Responses: Yes, 60%; No, 26%

Question: Do you think increasing your savings as much as possible in times of inflation is a good idea or a bad idea?
Responses: Good idea, 69%; Bad idea, 24%

In this respect there was a substantial change from earlier times when it was more generally thought that saving was a good idea; still, in 1979 only one-fourth of respondents changed this belief. (We should note that the question specifically referred to inflation.)

Question: Some people say that in times of inflation it's better to take on as much debt as possible, while others think that people should avoid taking on more debt. What do you think?
Responses: Better to take on debt, 14%; Avoid debt, 79%

Question: Some people think that the cost of borrowing money is high now, while others think it really is low considering inflation. Do you think interest rates are high, low, or about right considering inflation?
Responses: High, 54%; About right, 34%; Low, 3%

The small proportions saying that it is a good idea to go into debt during inflation may appear low, although a frequency of 14 percent of all respondents does represent a large number of families. Among families with an income of over $25,000, the proportion was much higher — 24 percent. Among these families, not fewer than 36 percent said that it is a bad idea to save during inflation.

The finding that very few respondents said that interest rates in 1979 were low considering inflation was more expected. Social learning is a slow, gradual process; too little time has passed with double-digit inflation to induce many people to call interest rates of 10 percent or more (that is, negative real interest rates) low.

Thus, there were substantial changes in the attitudes and beliefs of Americans in matters of inflation, and they contributed to the acceleration of inflation. Rather than being induced by inflation to save more, many Americans turned to buying in advance of further price increases. But it would be incorrect to assume that everyone's attitudes changed. In many respects, the notions of the great majority of Americans remained of a kind which may be thought to be helpful in fighting inflation.

The inflation survey of July–August 1979 contained the following question: "Would you say that on the whole you have been hurt by inflation, you have managed to stay even with inflation, or have you gotten a little bit ahead of inflation?" The responses are presented in Table 2.

Even among high-income families, among whom there

TABLE 2

Proportion of Family Units
Hurt by Inflation

Proportion saying...	All	Income under $10,000*	Income over $20,000**
Hurt by inflation	37%	39%	32%
Stayed even	48	53	47
Got ahead of inflation	12	5	19
Don't know	3	3	2
Total	100%	100%	100%

* Approximately one-fourth of all family units.
** Approximately one-third of all family units.

were very many whose recent gains in income had exceeded the price increases, less than one out of five said that they had gotten ahead of inflation, and one-third said that they had been hurt by inflation. The great majority said prices had increased more than their income over the preceding year, and only one in eight expressed the opinion that in the future their income would go up more than prices.

The opinions expressed about the financial damage caused by inflation may have been exaggerated. Aggregate real incomes advanced in 1977–78 and even in 1979 they declined only slightly, so that a substantial proportion of American families must have succeeded in gaining increases in wages, salaries, profits, etc., that were larger than the rate of inflation. But price increases occurred continuously and were salient and painful experiences whenever people went shopping. In contrast to the movement of prices, incomes normally increase occasionally rather than frequently. Moreover, income gains are usually viewed as personal accomplishments, so that even people with real income gains feel that they have been deprived by inflation of the well-deserved fruits of their labor or skill. Inflation, a development outside their control, is frequently seen by people as cheating them of what is rightfully theirs.

In view of these considerations, the finding must be emphasized that almost one-half of all Americans reported that they had stayed even with inflation and an additional 12 percent said they had gotten ahead of it. Among upper income Americans, two-thirds gave one of these two answers, rather than saying that they had been hurt by inflation.

Who are the people who reported having been hurt by inflation, and who are those who reported having stayed even or having gotten ahead of it? As can be seen from Table 2 there were some income differences: The frequency of "gotten ahead" answers was much larger among those with annual incomes of more than $20,000 than among those with lower incomes. Otherwise, differences based on income were small.

Surprisingly, the differences were also small between various age groups; even among those over 65, the majority said that they had stayed even. Education did make a difference: college graduates were more likely than others to say that they had gotten ahead of inflation. Regional differences in the answers were very small.

The answers to the "hurt/gotten ahead" question correlated strongly with the answers to a "better/worse off" question ("Would you say that you and your family are better off or worse off financially than you were a year ago."), but were far from being the same. Most of those who said they had been "hurt" professed to be worse off than a year earlier, and most of those who had "gotten ahead" said they were better off. But among those who said they had been hurt by inflation, 21 percent also felt they were better off financially; and among those who had gotten ahead as a result of inflation, 22 percent felt they were not better off. Among the many people who thought they had stayed even with inflation, as many as 45 percent also felt they were better off.

Extensive information on attitudes toward and behavior during inflation was also collected from a representative sample of businesses. Close to 1,000 managers of manufacturing, wholesale, and retail establishments were interviewed in the summer of 1979 (in a Survey Research Center study directed by Maureen Kallick). The answers to the question "hurt/stayed even/gotten ahead" — the same question that was asked of household family heads — were as follows when weighted by the size of employment:

The businesses were:	hurt by inflation	56%
	Stayed even	37
	Got ahead of inflation	7
		100%

These replies indicate that businesses succeeded less well than households in living with inflation. According to these

78

data, more businesses than households were hurt by inflation. This finding was rather surprising because at the same time many more managers professed that their businesses were better off rather than worse off compared to six months earlier, while for consumers it was the other way around. Apparently the stereotype "inflation is bad" strongly affected the responses by business managers.

This interpretation is borne out by the answers obtained to a different question in which business executives were asked not about their own firm, but rather about other American companies.

Question: Already we talked about whether your company has benefited from inflation or not. Thinking of the economy as a whole, about what percentage of companies in the U.S. do you think have benefited from inflation?
Responses: given by managers weighted by the size of employment of their establishment:

Proportion of American Companies Which Benefited

None	10%
1–10%	21
11–25%	19
26–50	15
51–100	9
Don't know	26
	100%

Disregarding the sizable group not answering the question, we find that one out of every eight business managers thought that one-half or more of all companies benefited from inflation, and one out of every three believed that one-third did so. It appears that it is easier to admit to beneficial effects of inflation when speaking of others than when reporting on one's own business.

In reply to several questions about how business executives proceeded in trying to cope with inflation, many highly revealing responses were obtained.

Question	Responses
Is your company making an effort. . .	
to pass on increases in costs more rapidly?	Yes, 55%; No, 45%
to set prices in anticipation of increases in costs?	Yes, 39%; No, 61%

Thus, strong evidence was obtained that many business firms practiced anticipatory pricing. Large manufacturing establishments appear to have done so most frequently, retailers least frequently.

In summary, the findings lead us to two major conclusions:

1. The impact of inflation in 1979 differed both among American households and among American businesses. Large proportions both of consumers and of businesses reported they had not been hurt by inflation.

2. Consumer and business behavior consisting of anticipatory buying and anticipatory pricing contributed greatly to the acceleration of inflation. Nevertheless, the old stereotype that inflation is evil remained powerful.

The change in people's attitudes toward inflation was not an isolated phenomenon. The breadth and depth of changing attitudes and beliefs were amply discussed in previous chapters in which the 1970s were characterized as representing a new economic era. Confidence, optimism, and understanding of economic trends were replaced by lack of confidence, confusion, and uncertainty. The belief in continuous betterment and growth gave way to a scaling down of expectations.

The lowering of expectations has become a worldwide phenomenon. Even in West Germany, with its strong currency and limited inflation and where attitudes toward the government hardly worsened, the belief in a further betterment and growth was severely shaken. What happened in Western Europe has been described as "bumping along around a low-growth trend." In the United States, as late as the summer of 1972, 50 percent of Americans expected to be better off financially in five years' time and only 6 percent expected to be worse off. (Most of the rest thought their economic situation would not change; some people refused to speculate about the distant future.) By the summer of 1979, however, only 34 percent of Americans said "We'll be better off in five years," and as many as 25 percent thought they would be worse off.

Fighting Inflation

There is no doubt that most people consider inflation an evil. In the late 1970s many more Americans said that inflation was the most serious problem confronting them. When asked which causes more serious hardship, inflation or unemployment, about two-thirds of the respondents in 1979 named inflation and one-fourth mentioned unemployment. This despite the fact that, as we have just shown, very many Americans did not feel hurt by inflation.

The main reason for the necessity to fight inflation lies not in the widely held belief that it is evil but rather that it is unjust and creates uncertainty, which in turn disrupts orderly economic activities. When two-digit inflation endures for some time and the belief is widespread that nothing can be done to slow it down, many people are preoccupied with trying to "stay even," rather than with doing the best job they are capable of. Productivity suffers, while speculation flourishes.

A decline in average real incomes or in the value of average assets is not an inevitable consequence of inflation. While certain assets such as bank deposits lose value if expressed in terms of their purchasing power, other assets and especially the largest asset of American families, the owner-occupied home, gain in value at times of inflation.[3] To be sure, for most people it is difficult if not impossible to make use of such gains. At the same time, young families suffer: Would-be buyers of first homes, who have no house to sell, are finding it harder and harder to achieve their cherished goal.

The psychological climate underlying our inflationary age

is supported by certain institutional developments. As Arthur M. Okun pointed out (in Brookings Reports, 1979), pricing by business firms has become increasingly related to change in cost rather than to fluctuations in demand. Wage increases were seen as a matter of equity and were demanded without regard to their consequences. Thus, a wage-price spiral was perpetuated.

"Indexation" — that is, linking wages, salaries, interest rates, and so forth with the cost of living — may not represent a solution. To be sure, it is justified in the case of income taxes, the present system being patently unjust in that higher incomes are taxed at a higher rate even when they have just kept pace with price increases. More generally, indexation can never be prompt and all-encompassing. It precipitates the belief that inflation will continue, does not remove the uncertainty about what one can and what one cannot afford to spend, and encourages speculation.

Increasing interest rates to high levels, a practice pursued by the Federal Reserve System, may be justified for the sake of defending the dollar but may not represent an effective weapon against inflation. Frequently rising interest rates generate the expectation of further increases and thus induce speculators to step up their borrowing before interest rates go still higher. Accumulation of inventories by business firms and purchases of houses and durables by consumers stem from motivational forces that are powerful in inflationary times and are not greatly deterred by high interest rates. At the same time, these high rates are often counterproductive. For most businesses, interest is an item of cost that is passed on in higher prices. In addition, some business investments greatly needed to improve productivity may be discouraged by high interest rates. Finally, rising interest rates are generally viewed as indicating bad times and raise the expectation of a recession.[4]

It has become quite obvious that fighting inflation is very difficult, especially in view of the experience with price and wage guidelines introduced by President Carter in the fall of 1978. The difficulties have frequently been attributed to selfishness as being a much more powerful motivational force than altruism. Some newspaper articles have referred to the growing spread of a "me too" psychology, implying that everybody was fighting for his or her personal advantage irrespective of the consequences of these actions on others and on the country. Buying in advance, anticipatory pricing, and demanding large increases in wages and salaries have been described as expressions of a growing emphasis on self-interest.

Self-interest alone represents an incomplete and misleading characterization of people's actions. What is in question is a restricted and short-run view as against a broad and long-run view of the entire situation. Business, for example, in setting prices as high as market conditions allow, and labor leaders, in demanding the highest possible wages, have failed to see the whole situation and the damage caused to themselves as well as others by rapidly rising prices and wages.[5]

It is justified to demand and fight for equitable treatment, but the definition of what is equitable remains in question. Equity is not the same as getting ahead in the game, and is not even the same as keeping the position that one has attained. To see what is required in a given situation and then to act accordingly should be understood to be equitable, even though some situations may call for actions that appear to represent a sacrifice over the short run.

In 1979 mandatory price and wage controls to insure the same treatment for all were frequently mentioned as an alternative to guidelines. But the position of President Carter that all-encompassing price and wage controls were not feasible in 1978–79 was justified both on economic and psychological grounds. Important segments of prices and costs, primarily those for energy, were determined at that time by foreign interests. Furthermore, price control works best with administered prices set by the sellers, while in sectors of the economy dominated by changes in supply and demand — especially agricultural prices — rationing alone can make price control effective when supplies decline due to natural causes. Finally, rationing and price control as well are effective and enforceable only when the people accept them and cooperate with them willingly. Price control may be evaded in a variety of ways, and when this is done by very many people the government is powerless. In 1978–79 the climate required for effective price control did not exist.[6]

This author published a little book shortly after Pearl Harbor, entitled *War Without Inflation* (Katona, 1942), in which he argued that World War II could be the first great war in history fought without substantial inflation. Not only was the knowledge of the needed economic and administrative measures available at that time, but the psychological conditions for approval of and cooperation with such measures were also present. Helping the war effort was something done willingly and was not seen as a sacrifice. The book implied that inflation might come after the end of the war, when patriotic fervor would vanish and measures taken against violators of controls might fail because of widespread evasion. A sharper contrast could hardly be imagined than that between the attitudes prevailing during World War II and during the 1970s.

No doubt, the circumstances that in 1979 would have disrupted effective mandatory controls of prices and wages also made cooperation with voluntary guidelines difficult. At a time when gasoline, fuel oil, electricity, and meat prices rose sharply, a 7 percent wage-increase appeared inadequate. But at the same time, as mentioned before, most Americans recognized that inflation was the greatest problem confronting them. Nevertheless, many people failed to understand that the success of wage and price guidelines could provide an alternative to continuous rapid inflation, and many even joked about another failure of Carter's policies, not recognizing the damage being done to the country as a whole. Failure to recognize the presence of an oil crisis reflected similar attitudes.

Least reassuring was the absence of any proposal about or thought of a compromise on the part of some labor leaders, many businessmen, and the government as well. Congress failed to consider the President's proposal to grant tax advantages to workers and employees who would accept moderate wage increases. The idea of relaxing wage guidelines at a time of substantial increases in the prices of energy and food, with the assurance of strengthening them at a later time in the absence of such price increases, was never proposed. The possibility of adding "teeth" to the voluntary guidelines and instituting mandatory price controls applied to certain areas where they would be enforceable because there were only a few sellers was hardly even discussed.

It might be considered paradoxical that mandatory price and wage controls are thought to be unworkable in the absence of a supportive psychological climate, while at the same time voluntary guidelines are considered feasible. In fact, the breakdown of a law — whether of liquor sales during prohibition or mandatory price and wage controls — is intolerable. On the other hand, voluntary guidelines are intended to restrict rather than prohibit action contrary to public interest. Guidelines and their application can be flexible. Even a clear violation of guidelines, say, by a labor union contract, might do little damage if it is publicly deplored and considered to be an unfortunate exception. The violation of guidelines by one or two business firms, if publicly castigated, might even do good rather than harm.

The need to change the current inflationary psychology has been much discussed. Arthur Burns, former head of the Federal Reserve Board, in an address delivered in Belgrade to bankers from all over the world, said: "If the United States and other industrial countries are to make real headway in the fight against inflation, it will first be necessary to rout the inflationary psychology" (quoted from an article by James

Reston in the *New York Times*, October 14, 1979). Having paid lip service to the basic need for such a "rout," he proceeded to propose monetary and fiscal policies with no reference to their psychological effect.

What possibilities are there to change the psychological climate fostering inflation? Persuasion alone is not sufficient. Even the most forceful addresses and speeches by leaders may fail to alter deep-seated beliefs that are reinforced by word of mouth. Changes in economic attitudes, expectations, and aspirations of very many people are not capricious; they are grounded in perceptions of economic trends. Yet a change in sentiment is not an automatic consequence of a change in economic trends. A slower rate of inflation or an upturn in the rate of production cannot assure the return of confidence unless, at the same time, some radical action is taken and is seen by the people as being both powerful and useful. However, the difficulties in changing underlying attitudes represent but one side of the coin. The notion that the current skeptical and antagonistic climate and the crisis of confidence are permanent features of our life is as unwarranted as trust in easy remedies. To be sure, early in 1980, when this book went to press, it appeared likely that the 1979 summer of discontent would be replaced by a 1980 summer of crisis. Furthermore, the roots of discontent go back many years. The crisis of confidence, the confusion, and the uncertainty all originated in the experiences of Vietnam and Watergate. Nevertheless, attitudes change, and even values are not permanent.

In 1979–80 the onset of a recession may serve to slow down inflation to some degree, but would hardly suffice to do the job. Even if many people would be compelled to reduce their spending by a decline in real income, the effect would not be the same and not as enduring as if they were to give up all spending motivated by an awareness or expectation of inflation. The very low saving rate that prevailed in America in 1979 (4.5 percent in 1979 and 3.3 percent in the fourth quarter of that year) indicates that in this respect there has as yet been little change; very many people have remained spending-minded. Installment credit continued to grow rapidly in the fall of 1979. Moreover, the expectation of and even the experience of a recession often prevail at the same time as the expectation of inflation. "Generalization of affect" is the name the author gave to a frequent phenomenon described in an earlier book (see Katona, 1964): One form of bad (or good) news adds to people's readiness to expect other bad (or good) developments.

This is not the place to enumerate the multitude of forms that an anti-inflationary economic policy might take. A strengthening of wage-price guidelines, the introduction of enforceable mandatory price controls for a few crucial products, and substantial tax advantages granted to saving might be part of that policy, as might the establishment of labor-business councils with some power and great moral influence. What is necessary is that the new policies catch the public imagination and create an atmosphere of confidence that they will succeed. Only then can they possibly be seen as representing a new start, terminating the era of the 1970s. It remains to be seen whether the international crises of 1980 or whether the presidential election of that year will make the accomplishment of this goal more difficult or easier.

Notes

1. In 1979–80, as is well known, gold prices skyrocketed to over $800 an ounce.

2. In the following report of survey data collected in July and August 1979, we abstain from quoting such uninteresting answers as "same," "don't know," etc., so that the quoted figures do not add up to 100 percent.

3. Data obtained in the Survey Research Center's longitudinal study of 5,000 American families, directed by James N. Morgan,

indicate that on the whole Americans are well aware of the rapid rise in the value of their homes. In 1977 (prior to the big advances in house prices in 1978), the average home owner who did not move estimated the value of his house as 57 percent higher than he did in 1972. The Consumer Price Index rose by 45 percent in those years. Bureau of the Census data indicate a 66 percent gain in the price of the average *new* house sold.

4. These arguments against raising interest rates are not contradicted by the well-justified view that, in 1979, 10 or even 14 percent interest charges represented a low rather than a high cost for money. Since the real value of money declines in times of rapid inflation, the lender should charge interest in the form of the rate of inflation plus, say, 3 percent, and therefore more than was charged in 1979 for business credit or mortgage and installment loans. As shown before, very few people have accepted this argument and most people felt hurt by the high interest rates. Borrowing funds for several years at, say, 15 percent may prove expensive if in future years the rate of inflation should be much smaller than in 1979.

5. The difference between the two kinds of consideration may also be expressed by the difference between preferences and values. Of course, all of us prefer to receive more rather than less. But behavior is also governed by the values we hold. Value is a relatively permanent conception, explicit or implicit, of the desirable (see Kluckhohn, 1951; Rokeach, 1973; Strumpel, 1976; and Smith, 1979), and desirable values are seen as "intrinsically required" or as "inherent in the object" (see Köhler, 1938; also Asch, 1952). Only in the theories of those who hold radical behavioristic views (e.g., Skinner, 1971) are values thought to be derived from habits and preferences. "Requiredness" is different from being compelled by law or custom; we are aware of it in all walks of life as the right course of action and as residing in the objective rather than the subjective environment. That absence of rapid inflation is a good thing is not just a personal preference by individuals. Many people are aware of the value of stability in economic trends and the absence of uncertainty generated by continuous large price increases.

6. Interestingly, the American people appeared to be aware of the difficulties of mandatory control. In the summer of 1979, somewhat less than 30 percent said that price controls would help to

fight inflation and more than 40 percent said that they would not. Thus, widespread doubts about price and wage controls appear to have grown due to the disappointment following Nixon's efforts in 1971–73.

Bibliography

Asch, Solomon E. *Social Psychology.* Englewood Cliffs: Prentice Hall, 1952.

Atkinson, John W. *An Introduction to Motivation.* Princeton: Van Nostrand, 1964.

————, and Feather, N.T. *A Theory of Achievement Motivation.* New York: Wiley, 1966.

Baerwaldt, Nancy, and Morgan, James N. "Trends in Intrafamily Transfers." In *Surveys of Consumers, 1971–72,* edited by Lewis Mandell, et al. Ann Arbor: Institute for Social Research, 1973.

Bowen, Howard R. *The Business Enterprise as a Subject for Research.* New York: Social Science Research Council, 1955.

Bronowski, Jacob. *Science and Human Values,* rev. ed. New York: Harper and Row, 1965.

————. *A Sense of the Future: Essays in Natural Philosophy.* Cambridge, Mass.: MIT Press, 1977.

Burns, Arthur. Quoted in article by James Reston, *New York Times,* October 14, 1979.

Duesenberry, James S. Comment in *Demographic and Economic Change in Developed Countries,* Universities-National Bureau of Economic Research. Princeton: Princeton University Press, 1960.

Duncan, Greg J., and Morgan James N., eds. *Five Thousand American Families — Patterns of Economic Progress,* Vol. 4, 1976; Vol. 5, 1977; Vol. 6, 1978. Ann Arbor: Institute for Social Research.

————, and Hill, Daniel. "Attitudes, Behavior and Economic Outcomes: A Structural Equations Approach." In *Five Thousand American Families — Patterns of Economic Progress,* Vol. 3, edited by Greg J. Duncan and James N. Morgan. Ann Arbor: Institute for Social Research, 1975.

Federal Reserve Bank of St. Louis. *Review,* June 1976.

Friedman, Milton. *Theory of the Consumption Function,* National Bureau of Economic Research. Princeton: Princeton University Press, 1957.

————. Nobel Lecture: "Inflation and Unemployment." *Journal of Political Economy,* 85, 3, 1977, 451–472.

Granovetter, Mark. *Getting a Job.* Cambridge: Harvard University Press, 1974.

Jacoby, Jacob; Chestnut, Robert; and Silverman, William. "Consumer Use and Comprehension of Nutrition Information." *Journal of Consumer Research,* 4, 1977, 119–128.

————; Olson, Jerry; and Haddock, Rafael. "Price, Brand Name, and Product Composition Characteristics as Determinants of Perceived Quality." *Journal of Applied Psychology,* 55, 1971, 570–579.

————; Szybillo, George; and Busato-Schach, Jacqueline. "Information Acquisition Behavior in Brand Choice Situations." *Journal of Consumer Research,* 3, 4, 1977, 209–216.

Juster, F. Thomas. "Inflation and Consumer Savings Behavior." Unpublished manuscript, University of Michigan, Survey Research Center, 1975.

————, and Wachtel, Paul. "Inflation and the Consumer." *Brookings Papers on Economic Activity*, 1, 1972, 71–114.

————, and Wachtel, Paul. "Uncertainty, Expectations, and Durable Goods Demand Models." In *Human Behavior in Economic Affairs*, edited by Burkhard Strumpel, James N. Morgan, and Ernest Zahn. New York: Elsevier, 1972.

Kahneman, Daniel, and Tversky, Amos. "On the Psychology of Prediction." *Psychological Review, 80*, July, 1973, 237 ff.

Katona, George. *War Without Inflation: The Psychological Approach to Problems of War Economy*. New York: Columbia University Press, 1942.

————. *Psychological Analysis of Economic Behavior*. New York: McGraw-Hill, 1951.

————. "Attitude Change: Instability of Response and Acquisition of Experience." *Psychological Monographs, 72*, 1958, 1–38.

————. *The Powerful Consumer*. New York: McGraw-Hill, 1960.

————. "The Relationship Between Psychology and Economics." In *Psychology: A Study of a Science*, Vol. 6, edited by S. Koch, 1963, 639–676.

————. *The Mass Consumption Society*. New York: McGraw-Hill, 1964.

————. *Private Pensions and Individual Saving*. Ann Arbor: Institute for Social Research, 1965.

————. "Theory of Expectations." In *Human Behavior in Economic Affairs*, edited by B. Strumpel, J.N. Morgan & E. Zahn. Amsterdam: Elsevier, 1972.

————. *Psychological Economics*. New York: Elsevier, 1975.

————. "Discussion." *American Economic Review Papers and Proceedings, 68*, 2, 1978, 75–76.

————. "Toward a Macropsychology." *American Psychologist, 34,* 2, 1979, 118–126.

————, and Mueller, Eva. "A Study of Purchase Decisions." In *Consumer Behavior,* edited by L. Clark. New York: New York University Press, 1954.

————; Strumpel, Burkhard,; and Zahn, Ernest. *Aspirations and Affluence.* New York: McGraw-Hill, 1971.

————, and Strumpel, Burkard. *A New Economic Era.* New York: Elsevier, 1978.

Keynes, John Maynard. *The General Theory of Employment, Interest, and Money.* New York: Harcourt, Brace, 1936.

Kluckhohn, Clyde. "Values and Value Orientations in the Theory of Action." In *Toward a General Theory of Action,* edited by T. Parsons and E. A. Shils. Cambridge, Mass.: Harvard University Press, 1951.

Köhler, Wolfgang. *The Place of Value in a World of Facts.* New York: Liveright, 1938.

Lancaster, Kevin. "A New Approach to Consumer Theory." *Journal of Political Economy, 74,* April, 1966, 132–157.

————. *Consumer Demand: A New Approach.* New York: Columbia University Press, 1971.

Lazarsfeld, Paul F.; Berelson, Bernard; and Gaudet, Hazel. *The People's Choice,* 2nd ed. New York: Columbia University Press, 1948.

Lewin, Kurt; Dembo, Tamara; Festinger, Leon; and Sears, P. S. "Level of Aspiration." In *Personality and Behavior Disorders,* edited by J. M. Hunt. New York: Ronald Press, 1944.

Machlup, Fritz. *Methodology of Economics and Other Social Sciences.* New York: Academic Press, 1978.

Maynes, E. Scott, et al. "The Local Consumer Information System:

An Institution-to-Be." *Journal of Consumer Affairs, 11,* Summer 1977, 17–33.

Miller, Arthur H. "Political Issues and Trust in Government: 1964–1970." *American Political Science Review, 68,* September, 1974.

Morgan, James N. "Consumer Investment Expenditures." *American Economic Review, 48,* 1958, 874–902.

———. "An Economic Theory of the Social Security System and Its Relation to Fiscal Policy." In *Income Support Policies for the Aged,* edited by G. S. Tolley and Richard Burkhauser. Cambridge, Mass.: Ballinger, 1976.

———. "Myth, Reality, Equity and the Social Security System." *Economic Outlook USA, 4,* Autumn 1977, 58–60.

———. "Intra-Family Transfers Revisited: The Support of Dependents Inside the Family." In *Five Thousand American Families,* Vol. 6, edited by Greg J. Duncan and James N. Morgan. Ann Arbor: Institute for Social Research, 1978.

———. "Multiple Motives, Group Decisions, Uncertainty, Ignorance, and Confusion: A Realistic Economics of the Consumer Requires Some Psychology." *American Economic Review Papers and Proceedings, 68,* 2, 1978, 58–63.

Newman, Joseph W., and Staelin, Richard. "Prepurchase Information Seeking for New Cars and Major Household Appliances." *Journal of Marketing Research, 9,* 1972, 249–257.

Rokeach, Milton. *The Nature of Human Values.* New York: Free Press, 1973.

Schumpeter, Joseph. *Das Wesen and Hauptinhalt der theoretischen Nationaloekonomie.* Leipzig: 1908.

Scitovsky, Tibor. *The Joyless Economy.* New York: Oxford University Press, 1976.

Sheppard, Harold, and Belitsky, A. H. *The Job Hunt.* Baltimore: Johns Hopkins Press, 1966.

Simon, Herbert A. *Models of Man.* New York: John Wiley & Sons, 1957.

————, and Newell, A. "Human Problem Solving." *American Psychologist, 26,* 1971, 145–159.

Skinner, Burrhus F. *Beyond Freedom and Dignity.* New York: Knopf, 1971.

Smith, M. Brewster. "Psychology and Values." *Journal of Social Issues, 34,* 4, 1978, 181–199.

Solomon, Richard L., and Corbit, John D. "An Opponent-Process Theory of Motivation." *American Economic Review, 68,* 6, 1978, 12–24.

Strumpel, Burkard. "Savings Behavior in Western Germany and the United States." *American Economic Review Papers and Proceedings, 65,* 2, 210–216.

————, ed., *Economic Means for Human Needs.* Ann Arbor: Institute for Social Research, 1976.

Tobin, James, and Dolbear, F. Trenery, Jr. "Comments on the Relevance of Psychology to Economic Theory and Research." In *Psychology: A Study of a Science,* vol. 6, edited by Sigmund Koch. New York: McGraw-Hill, 1963, 677–684.

Ward, Barbara. *Faith and Freedom: A Study of Western Society.* Westport, Conn.: Greenwood Press, 1954.

Wolgast, Elizabeth. "Economic Decisions in the Family." *Journal of Marketing, 23,* October, 1958, 151–158.

Zajonc, Robert G., and Burnstein, Eugene. "The Resolution of Cognitive Conflict Under Uncertainty." *Human Relations, 14,* 1961, 113–119.

Index